Douglas DC·8

By Terry Waddington

Great AIRLINERS SERIES

VOLUME TWO

About The Author

Terry Waddington is from England, and became interested in aviation during World War II when a relative gave him a collection of pre-war aircraft photos. He started his apprenticeship with Blackburn Aircraft in 1951, mostly working on the Beverley and Buccaneer. He moved to de Havilland Canada in 1963 to work on the DHC-5 design, then joined the DC-9 program at Malton in January 1964 as a sub-contractor liaison engineer. In 1966, he worked in the U.K. on the Lockheed C-5 wing design, then moved to Vancouver, Canada, in 1967 to work on the design of the CL-215 floats. Rejoining McDonnell Douglas at Long Beach in 1968, he worked on DC-8s and DC-9s as an engineer before transferring to Commercial Marketing in 1969. He was loaned to Irish Aerospace as V.P. Marketing at Shannon from 1985 to 1990 to lease MD-83s. He then joined GPA and retired after a heart transplant in 1991. Now living with his wife in Roseburg, Oregon, his main interest is collecting slides and aviation books, particularly anything to do with Douglas jetliners and British-built aircraft. He is a past president of both the Canadian and American Aviation Historical Societies.

Series Editor: Jon Proctor
Series Design: Nicholas A. Veronico

Cover design by Randy Wilhelm, Keokee Company, Sandpoint, Idaho
Copy Editors: Fred Chan, Billie Jean Plaster

Cover photos courtesy McDonnell Douglas Corporation
Unless otherwise indicated, non-credited photos are courtesy McDonnell Douglas Corporation

The *Great Airliners* series:
Volume One: *Convair 880/990* by Jon Proctor
Volume Two: *Douglas DC-8* by Terry Waddington
Volume Three: *Boeing 747SP* by Brian Baum

Published by

WORLD TRANSPORT PRESS, INC.

P.O. Box 521238
Miami, Fla. 33152-1238
Tel. +1 (305) 477-7163 Fax +1 (305) 599-1995

Table of Contents

Appendicies

ACKNOWLEDGEMENTS

The writer is indebted to many individuals who have contributed information to make this book possible. Many are former Douglas co-workers who were involved in the design and flight-testing of the DC-8. Foremost of these is Harry Gann who, though retired, still remains active in looking after the company's historical files on a voluntary basis. Harry patiently dug out many old brochures, specs and photos and gave me leads to other sources. I wish to thank the McDonnell Douglas Corporation, in particular Eric Macklin and Pat McGinnis, for access to Company photos and data used in this book. My gratitude goes to former DAC employees Bob Archer, Jim Burton, Gene Dubil, Ron Howell, Gerry Markgraf, Mike Machat, Don Mullin, John Rapillo, Roger Schaufele, among many who offered to supply assistance. Other help came from Swissair, United Airlines, Dr. James Young of the Air Force Flight Test Center and former FAA DC-8 Project Pilot Joe Tymczyszyn.

But the project would have been totally impossible without help from all the enthusiasts that I have traded slides with over the past 35 years, including Jeff Burch, Terry Coxall, Eddy Gual, Martin Hornlimann, Paul Huxford, Clay Jansson, Peter Keating, Eric Legendre, Jean Magendie, Malcolm Nason, Hans Oehninger, Mike Rathke, Harry Sievers, Bob Smith, Brian Stainer, Martin Stamm, John Wegg, Udo Weisse and Gary Vincent, to name but a few, plus the many people I have associated with at the annual and regional Airliners International conventions. My sincere apologies to those whose names are omitted. Jon Proctor also deserves special mention as book editor and guide.

I am particularly grateful to Donald W. Douglas Jr., son of the founder, and former president of Douglas Aircraft, for his insights into some of the more critical decisions affecting the DC-8. He was intimately associated with the airplane from its initial conception to the final delivery.

Lastly, I wish to thank my wife, Anne, for putting up with my hobby for the last 38 years, and leaving me in peace to write this volume. However, the dedication goes to the unknown English donor and his family who gave me a second chance. To them, I am eternally grateful. Most of the book royalties will be donated to the Harefield Hospital Heart Transplant Trust in his memory.

Terry Waddington
Roseburg, Oregon

H

Harefield Heart Transplant Trust

Author's Note

I make no apology for not including a more detailed individual history of the 556 DC-8s that were built. There were two reasons for this, the first being a lack of space, it being more important to set the development history down for the first time. Additionally, with so many DC-8s still active, such a listing would be obsolete before the book reached the printers. Annual DC-8 individual aircraft history reviews and monthly updates are to be found in the several excellent specialist publications listed in the Bibliography and marked with an asterisk.

INTRODUCTION

Ever since the first flight of the Wright brothers, on December 17,1903, aviation has been in a constant race to develop bigger, faster aircraft to fly longer ranges at more economical rates. The two world wars had much influence on the development of the airplane and its power plants and systems, but it was a select band of dedicated men, on both sides of the Atlantic, who were to see that the future of world development depended on speeding up communication through carrying people and cargo by air.

One of these pioneers was Donald Wills Douglas, a young man who enrolled as a cadet in the United States Naval Academy in 1909. In 1912, he became interested in aeronautical engineering and decided to move to the Massachusetts Institute of Technology, where an aeronautical engineering course was available. After graduation, noted pioneer Glenn L. Martin invited Douglas to work for him in Los Angeles. During World War I, he played the lead role in the design and development of the Martin MB-1 twin-engine bomber, an outstanding aircraft for its time. However, Douglas wanted to break out on his own and, with $600 in capital, set out to form a company in June 1920.

From then on, many types of Douglas aircraft were to grace the skies, including the Cloudster, the famous Around-the-World Cruisers, numerous military examples and, most noteworthy of all, the DC-1 through DC-7 series of commercial transports. A key feature of the development of Douglas design concepts became evident with the DC-1 through DC-3 series, in which a basic design was utilized to develop later models by stretching the fuselage, strengthening the wing and installing more powerful engines. This approach continued with the DC-4 through DC-7 series, which dominated the commercial airways in the late 1940s and throughout the 1950s.

With the coming of the jet age, Douglas was to continue the tradition with the DC-8, stretching it, increasing operating weights, modifying the wings and changing the engines. Even after production ceased in 1972, the inherent longevity built into the airframe allowed others to improve and modify the aircraft, ensuring its service for many years to come. Though delivered new to only 48 customers, the DC-8 has worn the colors of some 350 different operators to date and, with over 250 airframes still active, should expand that number considerably for many years to come.

Chapter I

Development

Artist's rendering of the original 1946 version of the DC-8 at the old Glendale, California Air Terminal.

The Stillborn DC-8

Toward the end of World War II, aircraft production was slowing down and military contracts were being cut back. As with the other major manufacturers, Douglas Aircraft Company, located at Santa Monica, California, put its advanced design team to work on aircraft to fill the perceived need of the airlines with the coming of peace.

Douglas was fortunate in that it already had some of the answers. Medium- and long-range markets could be handled by converting the C-54 which was already in production for the armed forces and possessing great development potential, in the Douglas tradition. The short-range market could be filled temporarily by the DC-3, but the type, already out of production, was considered too small for economic airline service. So it was in this area that design efforts were concentrated as the war ended.

In 1943, Douglas Chief Engineer Ed Burton had created the concept of a twin-engine bomber with exceptional payload-range capability, its low drag shape providing an excellent cruising speed of over 300 miles an hour. The XB-42, as it came to be known, was unique in that its power plants – 1,325 hp Allison V-1710-125s – were mounted in parallel just behind the cockpit. Power was transmitted to two contra-rotating propellers mounted in the tail-cone by a series of five shafts, leaving a very clean wing. By August 1944, two pro-

totypes had flown with excellent results. However, with the war's end in sight and the advent of jet-powered aircraft, the XB-42 was relegated to a test role with two small jet engines mounted under the wings.

Douglas utilized the XB-42 layout and performance data to produce a radical new approach to transport aircraft design. With the same power plant and installation method, a 48-seat airliner of exceptionally clean appearance emerged. It was claimed that this concept would reduce the overall drag coefficient by 25 percent compared with a conventional design of similar size. Other advantages included eliminating single engine-out control problems, easy access to the doors and safe access to the engines during ground test runs. Capable of carrying a 12,000-pound payload over a 300-mile stage-length, the aircraft had a planned Maximum Takeoff Weight (MTOW) of 39,500 pounds.

Low to the ground because of the absence of wing-mounted propellers, the DC-8 Airbus, as it was to be named, featured a tricycle undercarriage and a clean, straight-tapered wing which contained 1,000 gallons of fuel in tanks between the spars. The cabin floor was only five feet above the ground, facilitating the installation of folding airstairs with upward-opening passenger doors providing protection from the weather.

The engines were contained in a stainless steel box with full fire and vapor protection installed. Driveshafts located beneath the cabin floor drove two 15-foot diameter, three-bladed, contra-rotating propellers via a reduction box. To shorten ground roll-out, the propellers were to be reversible.

The cabin could be pressurized to provide a cabin altitude of 8,000 feet while operating at 20,000 feet. Passengers seats would be placed four- or five-abreast at a 36-inch, high-density seat pitch! Cargo storage was ahead of the passenger compartment, situated above the engines and also at the rear. A moveable bulkhead permitted various mixed cargo/passenger configurations to be created, with removed seat pads stowed in the overhead racks and the frames folded against the fuselage walls. The bulkhead could be moved to a maximum of 10 feet aft of the normal location, thus enlarging the cargo compartment from 234 to 321 cubic feet. This may have been the first real attempt to design a "quick change" interior. In parallel with the convertible DC-8, an all-cargo version was being offered, featuring a reinforced floor and large freight doors fore and aft.

The main engineering problem with this design centered around the extended shaft drive, which pushed development costs to a point where the sales price exceeded that of its competitors by over $100,000. Douglas made strenuous efforts to sell the DC-8, but airline managers were unsure of the Allison engines and the radical new design. Even the predicted performance and operating costs, which were half of those achieved by the DC-3, failed to win them over, and instead they selected the more conventional Convair 240 and Martin 2-0-2.

A First Look

At the end of the war, the paucity of military funding caused Douglas to redirect its efforts towards the commercial market. During the war, alongside the almost 11,000 DC-3s/C-47s produced, the four-engine C-54 entered service with nearly twice the speed, a considerable increase in range, and up to 70 seats. The C-54 was the military version of the DC-4, originally due to enter service with the airlines at the outbreak of the war. By the end of hostilities 1,165 C-54s had been built.

Douglas had large amounts of material available from canceled government contracts. As a result, the company quickly reverted to building the non-pressurized airliner version without the standard cargo door fitted to the C-54. The first new civilian DC-4 was delivered to Western Airlines in January 1946. Unfortunately sales were slow due to the availability of hundreds of low-priced surplus C-54s. Production ended with completion of the 79th aircraft. Additionally, Canadair built 71 DC-4Ms, a Rolls Royce Merlin-powered version, for three airlines, Trans-Canada Air Lines (TCA), Canadian Pacific Air Lines (CPA) and British Overseas Airways Corp. (BOAC), plus the Royal Canadian Air Force (RCAF).

Fortunately, the Douglas penchant for building development capability into a basic design was to manifest itself yet again. The company had always intended to pressurize the

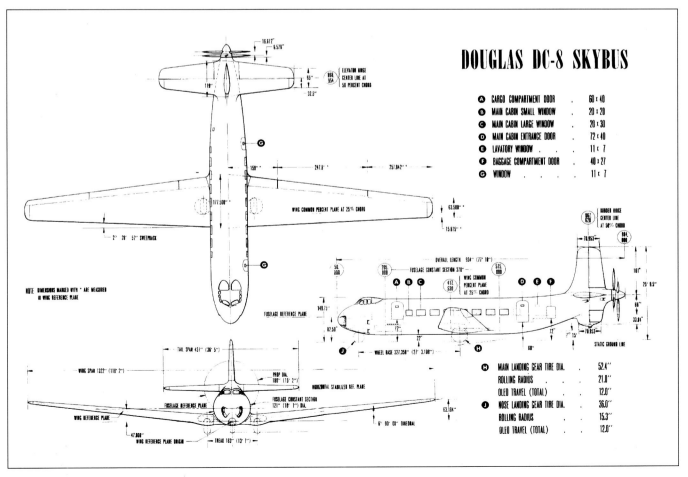

Artist's rendering from a Douglas brochure dated July 15, 1953.

DC-4 cabin, but the need for mass production had delayed the program. Faced with increasing competition from Lockheed's Constellation and the Boeing Stratocruiser, Douglas took advantage of a government funded C-54 development program to produce a pressurized and stretched version called the XC-112, featuring 2,100 hp Pratt & Whitney R-2800 engines.

The prototype flew on February 15, 1946, but lack of federal funding resulted in no immediate purchases by the U.S. military. This allowed Douglas to initiate a commercial program based on the same design. The resulting DC-6 became a great sales success. Over the next 22 years, 704 variants of the DC-6, DC-6A, DC-6B and military versions were produced, followed by the ultimate stretched version, the DC-7 series, of which 338 were built.

Douglas had begun looking at jet-powered airliners as far back as 1943, but the limited power and reliability of available engines precluded any real chance of development in the foreseeable future. The gigantic Douglas XB-19 four-engine bomber, which flew in June 1941, had shown that large aircraft — the wing span was 219 feet — could be flown as easily as smaller aircraft. With a range of 5,000 miles and payload of some 35,000 pounds, it demonstrated that intercontinental flights with sizable payloads were feasible.

In 1946, Douglas entered the jet era when it commenced flight testing a small, experimental twin-jet bomber, the XB-43. Based on the XB-42 previously mentioned, it was a natural progression of airframe development. Though the XB-43 proved to be very capable, it was dropped in favor of the four-engine North American B-45. Samples of both the XB-42 and XB-43 remain in the Smithsonian collection today.

The Douglas C-74 Globemaster I transport made its first flight in September 1945, but only 14 of the 50 originally ordered were delivered to the military. With a takeoff weight of 172,000 pounds, it was the biggest land-based aircraft to be ordered for mass production during the war. In 1945, Pan Am placed an order for 26 of the civilian version, to have been designated the DC-7. But the order was canceled in 1947, when it was considered too big for future traffic demands, and also became too expensive following the reduced Air Force order. The C-74 gained significance on November 18, 1949, when it flew from Mobile, Alabama to England with 103 passengers and crew, the first time an aircraft had crossed the Atlantic with more than 100 people aboard.

The Globemaster was replaced by the C-124, which first flew in 1949, and featured a much larger diameter fuselage and more powerful engines. All of this work increased the Douglas team's confidence that it could build large, dependable and economic aircraft. With the growing use of jet engines by the military, it became apparent to company engineers that this development would eventually spill over into commercial aviation.

In fact, by the end of 1949, two four-engine jet airliners were already flying. In England, de Havilland's prototype swept-wing deH.106 Comet first flew on July 27, followed closely by the Canadian-built Avro Canada C102 Jetliner's first flight on August 10. Initial orders for the Comet I had come from BOAC and British South American Airways as early as 1946, and others followed as the Comet prototype demonstrated its capabilities.

Before the year had ended, Canadian Pacific had signed up for two 48-seat examples and, by mid-1951, two other international airlines and, ironically, the RCAF had placed orders. The Avro Jetliner, with its more conventional straight wing, attracted only two serious potential customers, the U.S. Air Force, which wanted to use it as a navigation trainer, and Howard Hughes, on behalf of TWA. However, neither order materialized, probably due to politics, and the program was dropped in order to concentrate on the design of the Avro CF-105 Arrow all-weather jet fighter.

By the early 1950s, the Douglas Military Division at El Segundo, led by Ed Heinemann, began to amass a great deal of high speed and high altitude experience in jet- and rocket-powered flight via a series of experimental aircraft, the famous Skystreak and Skyrocket programs. The F3D Skynight, a twin-jet all-weather fighter developed for the U.S. Navy and U.S. Marines, was in quantity production by 1952 and later achieved fame as the first jet ever to shoot down another aircraft at night during the Korean War.

The bat-winged supersonic F4D Skyray, powered by the Pratt & Whitney J57, was approaching production status, giving Douglas familiarity with this engine which was to become the civilian JT3 series. Material development and manufacturing techniques were major activities undertaken in parallel with the development of high speed test vehicles. Titanium was used extensively for the first time in the design of the stiletto-shaped Douglas X-3 research aircraft. The A-3 Skywarrior being built for the U.S. Navy was significant as it provided experience with the use of jet engines in pods, mounted below a moderately swept wing.

A major influence on the design of this new breed of aircraft lay in the progress being achieved by the engine manufacturers. Thrust levels were increasing rapidly; fuel burns were being reduced and reliability was constantly improved through the use of new materials and design changes. In

1951, when the civilian Pratt & Whitney JT3 engine was being developed from the military J57, the feasibility of jet-powered airliners became more realistic. Piston engine development was tapering off as manufacturers concentrated resources in the development of bigger and more efficient jet engines and, to a lesser degree, turbo-props.

In 1952, the U.S. Air Force was beginning to consider a jet-powered replacement for its piston-powered KC-97 aerial refueling tanker. The specifications suggested that a spin-off commercial airliner could be a simple extension of the basic tanker requirement. This was, perhaps, a thinly veiled government effort to encourage American aircraft manufacturers to enter the jetliner market in competition with the British Comet. The military called for an aircraft with a 250,000-pound gross weight, able to operate at altitudes and speeds compatible with the B-47 and B-52 bombers. Available engine-thrust levels dictated a need for at least four power plants.

The Douglas advanced design team had for some time been looking at jetliner concepts. In June 1952, with no publicity, a formal project office was established at Santa Monica to address the military proposal and airline requirements. The company did not want to rush into the jet age and drain its assets because it still dominated the airliner market and had a very profitable backlog in excess of 275 DC-6s and DC-7s. Thus no real urgency was applied to the new program, designated as the DC-8.

At the time, the Santa Monica design team wrestled with a proposal for an outsized turbo-prop cargo aircraft, the C-132, for the U.S. Air Force. Don Douglas and his Vice President of Engineering, Arthur Raymond, were not totally convinced that airlines were ready for the jet era. The industry had invested over $1.5 billion on new piston-engine aircraft in recent years, which still needed to be written down.

Recently, C. R. Smith of American Airlines had personally asked Douglas for a faster version of the DC-6 to compete with the improved Super Constellation, and promised to make it worthwhile with a substantial order. At first reluctant to do this, Douglas had finally agreed and re-assigned manpower to design and produce the DC-7 series, which became highly successful and profitable. The production line at Santa Monica was delivering DC-6s, and eventually DC-7s, at a rate peaking at 18 aircraft per month. Because of American

Airlines' huge outlay for the DC-7, Smith was able to talk Mr. Douglas into delaying the DC-8 launch.

After talking to many potential customers, there was a wide divergence of opinion as to just what form the DC-8 should take. One group thought was it ought to be smaller than the Boeing entry, avoiding direct competition. But others, influenced by Pan Am, were pushing for a larger aircraft, powered by either six J-57 derivatives or four of the more powerful J-75s. The U.S. Navy was asking for a turbo-prop transport and an Airborne Warning and Command System (AWACS) aircraft, while American and United were both pressing Douglas to produce a turbo-prop airliner as the logical followup aircraft. Much thought was given to designing an airframe that could accept either type of engine, thus reducing development costs while still satisfying a wider spectrum of customers. There was a feeling in Douglas management that they were being caught in the middle because in parallel with the Boeing jetliner program, Lockheed was pursuing the turbo-prop market with what was to become the Electra airliner and Orion anti-submarine patrol plane for the Navy. The Douglas board of directors belatedly decided to concentrate on a specification similar to the Boeing design.

Led by Chief Project Engineer Ivor Shogrun, the Douglas team, after much pressure from Donald Douglas, Jr., began defining the parameters of field performance, runway length requirements, range, size, weight, passenger comfort, number and location of engines and, of course, cost. Hundreds of combinations of wing sweep, camber, span, thickness and airfoil shapes were examined in the wind tunnel. Crescent-shaped and delta wings were among the configurations considered. Much effort was expended in determining the location of the engines, not only from a weight and balance aspect, but also for maintenance accessibility. A podded engine design was finally selected in order to utilize the entire wing for fuel; the wheels were designed to fold up into the lower fuselage. In concert with this, the marketing department was looking at traffic demands, trying to forecast the quantity and size of new jetliners that would be needed over the next 20 years. All of this work was initially shrouded in secrecy, but by mid-1953, the project definition was firmed up and a full-size wooden mock-up had been created to show potential customers what the DC-8 would look like. From the very beginning, two basic models were shown to airline

DC-8 Model Comparision
(1953 Proposal)

		DC-8A DOMESTIC	DC-8A DOMESTIC	DC-8B DOMESTIC	DC-8B OVERWATER
Maximum take-off weight	(lb)	209.600	209.600	209.600	*209.000
					**248.000
Maximim Landing weight	(lb)	134.600	*140.900	136.000	*143.900
			***141.800		***146.700
Maximum Zero Fuel Weight	(lb)	121.401	*123.119	122.638	*125.923
			**123.859		***128.123
Manufacturer's Empty Weight	(lb)	93.920	*94.733	95.197	*97.537
			**95.473		***99.737
PAYLOAD					
Passenger Seats		80	76	80	76
Cargo Volume	(cuft)	1.090	1.090	1.090	1.090
Space Limit Payload	(lb)	24.100	23.440	24.100	23.410
Passengers (165lb each)		13.200	12.540	13.200	12.540
Cargo (10lbs per cuft)	(lb)	10.900	10.900	10.900	10.900
Weight Limit Payload	(lb)	24.100	23.440	24.100	23.440
Flight Crew		3	4	3	4
Cabin Crew		2	2	2	2
Fuel Capacity	(USG)	13.540	*13540	13.540	*13.540
			**15.380		***18.620
	(lb)	88.000	*88.000	88.000	*88.000
			**100.000		***121.000

* 13.540 USG fuel capacity - internal fuel only
** 15.380 USG fuel capacity- internal fuel plus two 470 USG underwing tanks
*** 18.620 USG fuel capacity- internal fuel plus two 875 USG underwing tanks

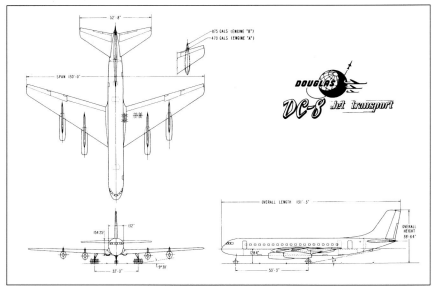

Three-view drawing, above, and sample seating lay-outs, opposite page, from the 1953 Douglas brochure. Note pylon mounted fuel tank planned for the DC-8 overwater version.

A variety of interior layouts was made available to the airlines. Typically, a standard 80-seat Domestic aircraft had four-abreast seating with a 40-inch pitch, plus a spacious lounge for seven people, located aft. This 40-inch pitch set the spacing of the large triple-pane windows which was to remain standard on all future DC-8 passenger models. With the removal of the lounge, and substituting a "three and two" five-abreast configuration, defined as "coach" class, capacity increased to 110, still at the 40-inch pitch! Both versions featured three lavatories, stationed against the rear pressure dome. The galley, with its own service door, was located on the starboard side, opposite the rear entry door.

The Overwater model came in a 76-seat layout, with a slightly smaller lounge, but a large "cloakroom" was included. Two lavatories were located aft, with a separate small washroom for men and a large powder room for the ladies. A considerably larger galley was included to handle the additional in-flight service needs. All versions were to fly with a flight crew of three pilots plus two flight attendants.

The aircraft was intended to cruise at 540 mph, with a 23,440-pound payload, (typically 76 passengers and 10,900 pounds of cargo). The range varied from 3,000 miles for the DC-8A (Domestic) to 4,000 miles with a full payload for the DC-8B (Overwater). New York-to-Los Angeles could be flown in 5 hours, 35 minutes, the return journey being 4 hours, 30 minutes. The trans-Atlantic New York-London segment could be flown nonstop in 6 hours, 45 minutes. On the return journey, the DC-8A required a fuel stop because of prevailing headwinds, but the DC-8B had no such restrictions.

Meanwhile, Boeing had begun building a company-funded prototype, initially investing some $16 million of its own funds in the project. Few details were released until the Boeing 367-80 rolled out on May 14, 1954, followed by a first flight on July 15.

Art Raymond, at an address to the Swedish Aeronautical Society in September 1954, stated, "The success of the American efforts to meet the challenge of British jetliner competition may ultimately hinge on U.S. government orders for military counterparts of currently projected civilian jet transports." He also revealed that up to that point, Douglas had invested 250,000 man-hours and over $3 million of company funds in the DC-8 project. Don Mullin, who flew the company team to Dayton to hand over the Douglas aerial tanker proposals, recalls Mr. Douglas stating that the Company's future was riding on the aircraft.

With regard to the military requirement, the general feeling at Douglas was that the government would buy a jet tanker from more than one manufacturer. This attitude was probably based on the previous purchase of transport aircraft of similar capability from both Douglas (C-54, C-118) and Lockheed (C-69 and C-121). At the outbreak of the Korean conflict, Douglas Sr. had been called to Washington and

management, the DC-8A, offered for 1956 delivery and the DC-8B, which would be available in 1958. Interestingly, security restrictions at the time precluded Douglas from disclosing which engines were to be offered. Brochures of that period describe the engines simply as "Engine A" and "Engine B." In hindsight, we know that "A" was the Pratt & Whitney J57 and "B" the more powerful J75. Two variants of each model were offered, Domestic and Overwater. In each case, airframes and engines were identical, the primary difference being Operating Empty Weights (OEW) and internal fuel capacities. Additionally, the Overwater version had a navigator's position and life rafts, etc. This nomenclature was used in-house to describe all the passenger versions up to and including the Series 50s. The DC-8A had a 209,600-pound MTOW, compared with 248,000 pounds for the DC-8B. Overwater versions required the use of additional fuel tanks of either 470- or 875-gallon capacity, pylon-mounted beneath each outer wing.

The 130-foot wing, with a 30-degree sweep-back at quarter chord, had an area of 2,600 square feet. Overall length was 131 feet, 4 inches, with a height of 39 feet, 7 inches. The main landing gear consisted of four wheels on each strut, mounted on a common axle. To stow the wheels in the lower fuselage, the oleos rotated 90 degrees. The steerable nose gear was a twin-wheeled unit. The fuselage cross-section (maximum width 132 inches) was a "double-bubble" configuration developed to solve two requests from the customer airlines. Maximum cabin width at shoulder height was requested for comfort, and a big increase in head-room in the baggage compartment would eliminate the requirement for baggage handlers to crawl in on their backs to stow cargo, which was the case on earlier Douglas designs. Two intersecting circle segments, meeting at the floor line, resolved both design parameters. When the fuselage width was increased to allow six-across seating, this cross-section became much more pronounced because the lower segment remained unchanged.

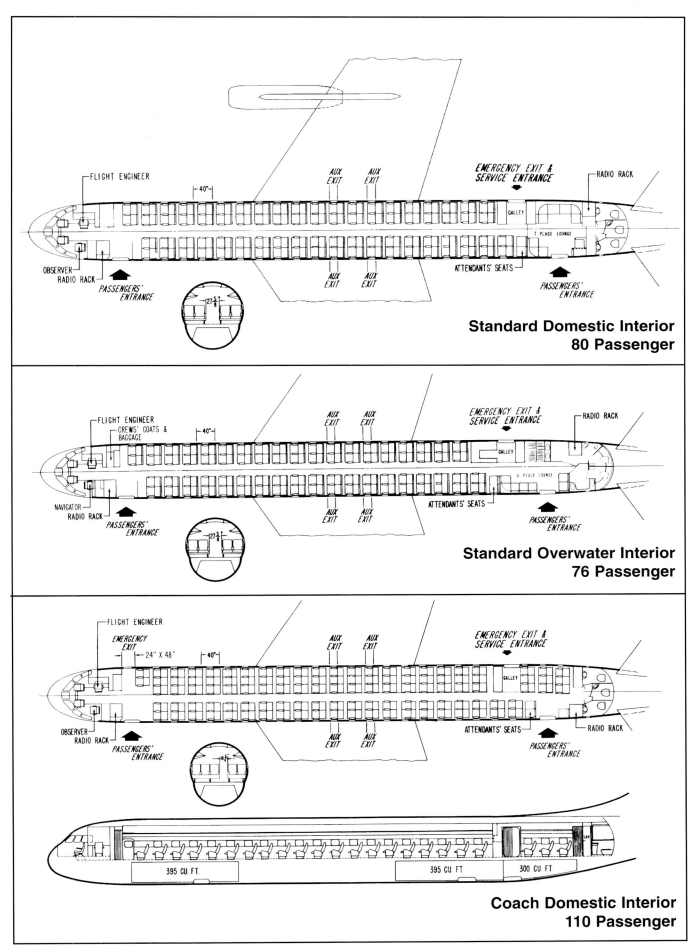

**Standard Domestic Interior
80 Passenger**

**Standard Overwater Interior
76 Passenger**

**Coach Domestic Interior
110 Passenger**

asked to put the C-54 back into production. He pointed out to Secretary of the Air Force Harold E. Talbot that the C-118 was already being produced and further suggested that, to maintain fair commercial competition, similar orders should be placed for the Lockheed C-121. Talbot concurred and brought in the president of Lockheed, who was waiting in the outer office, giving him an order!

So it came as a great shock, then, in February 1955, when Talbot, pushed by General Curtis E. LeMay, abruptly awarded Boeing a contract for 21 KC-135s before the competitive bids were completed. This decision was prompted by increased urgency to replace the KC-97 as the Strategic Air Command's fleet refueller when the Cold War intensified. The Boeing entry was clearly available at least a year ahead of its competitors. As a result of this initial order, Boeing was able to recover a great deal of its start-up costs. In effect, Douglas had to price its aircraft based on a package starting at Ship One, whereas Boeing's prices were based on Ship 22 onwards. This gave Boeing a tremendous unit price advantage.

Mr. Douglas personally appealed the decision in Washington to high-level politicians and civil servants at great length, but to no avail; it was a "done deal," and undoubtedly the largest, single blow ever to befall the Company, affecting its financial well-being for years to come.

Decision Time

In spite of its loss of the military tanker program, Douglas realized that it had to go on with the DC-8 design to avoid getting too far behind the Boeing lead. The basic design was revisited and many more detailed discussions were held with key Douglas customers in an attempt to arrive at a consensus on the basic design concept and related details.

Mock-ups play an important part in aircraft design, and great use of this aid was made to develop cockpit and cabin interiors. Much debate raged back and forth over the cabin cross-section, and whether to seat passengers five- or six-abreast. A number of small cross-section examples were used to resolve the cabin width. United even built its own mockup to arrive at the right size, working in conjunction with the manufacturer. United President William A. "Pat" Patterson was a strong proponent of the six-abreast layout, and as United was considered to be a primary launch customer, the upper fuselage diameter was increased to 147 inches.

Douglas built a complete replica of the DC-8 in the summer of 1955. It was used by engineers to develop not only the interior layouts, but also to determine the exact location of major items such as pumps, electronic "black boxes," ducting, wire bundles and cable routing. Even the exterior was painted in Douglas house colors. This mockup alone cost $7.5 million, but they felt it saved at least $15 million in the long run.

The increased cross-section led to a stretching of the fuselage, and a much larger wing which was required to keep wing-loading within reason and to carry more fuel. Larger tail surfaces, with more sweep-back on the fin, were also designed.

On June 7, 1955, Donald Douglas, Sr., facing one of his most critical decisions, announced that Douglas would build the DC-8 as a private venture. The company anticipated that it would cost in the region of $450 million by the time the first aircraft was delivered, becoming the largest privately financed venture by a single company at the time. It is worth mentioning that, if Douglas had won a share in the U.S. Air Force tanker program, it would have received around $100 million in governmental funding to help offset develop costs.

The formal announcement stated that the first flight would take place in December 1957, with initial airline deliveries slated for 1959. To reduce costs and speed up the program, they decided to dispense with a prototype and use the first eight aircraft off the assembly line for flight testing. Aircraft specifications included a wing span of 134 feet, 6 inches, length of 140 feet, 6 inches and a height of 40 feet, 2 inches. The domestic airplane, powered by J-57 (later called JT3) engines, would weigh in at 211,000 pounds, while the long range version, powered by the J-75 (later re-designed JT4) would have a 257,000-pound gross weight. Passenger capacity had increased to a 125-seat, single-class layout, still using the 40-inch seat pitch as standard. The cruise range had improved to 3,700 miles for the long-range example. The domestic version was to be the first type available.

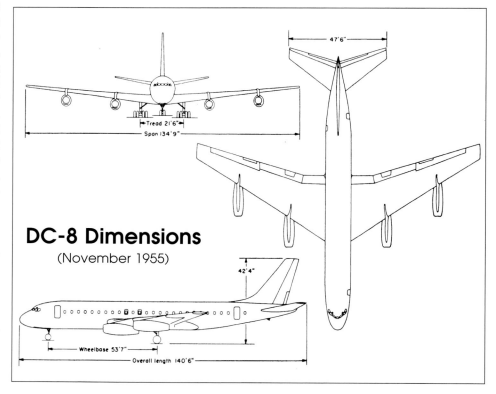

DC-8 Dimensions
(November 1955)

Interestingly, Boeing did not elect to offer the more powerful J-75, but initially standardized on the J-57. The 707 was much lighter and somewhat smaller than the DC-8 Overwater version, with a MTOW of 235,000 pounds. Fuel capacity was 16,848 gallons, compared to 18,538 gallons in the DC-8.

Aerodynamics engineers decided to use a development of a 20-year old National Advisory Committee for Aeronautics airfoil which would give high-speed characteristics with a moderate 30 degree sweep-back, reduced from an earlier 35-degree sweep design. The objective was to have similar characteristics to the DC-7 during the slower speeds of the takeoff and landing, simplifying crew transition from pistons to jets. It was predicted that on the downwind leg, speeds would be identical and base legs actually slower. The stall speed was only 5 knots above the DC-7 at 90 knots with a 50-degree flap setting.

From the beginning, the constant-section fuselage was designed to permit future stretch versions as more powerful engines became available. The wing was also engineered to allow bigger engines to be fitted without changes to the structure. Structural design of the DC-8 was aimed at minimizing the risk of catastrophic failure by using several design tenets, including: multiple member structures; retention of a large percentage of the initial strength after the failure of any one element; and restriction of the extent of the failure. To ensure cabin pressure integrity, all the external doors were plug-type to prevent blowing out. The doors opened inward, swinging outboard on a double-pin arrangement. Each would be wider than the opening. Cabin pressurization was provided by several units, any two of which could provide reasonable ventilation while the aircraft descended.

Sales discussions with the airlines were intensified immediately. Prior to the formal announcement, no real negotiations had taken place with regard to price and delivery schedules. On October 13, 1955, Pan American President Juan Trippe announced the purchase of 25 JT4-powered Overwater versions of the Douglas DC-8 in conjunction with an order for 20 Boeing 707s. The Douglas order was worth in excess of $160 million, including spares. Douglas got the larger order based on its reputation and the slightly larger fuselage cross-section. A fallout from this was, of course, that Boeing had to re-design the cabin of the Boeing 707 for the commercial market because the prototype Dash 80 had the equivalent of a five-abreast seating cross-section. Pan Am, the launch customer for the DC-8, accepted that it would not receive the first deliveries because Pratt & Whitney was offering the JT3 for earlier delivery than the JT4. However, its order for 707s would allow a very early entry into the jet travel market. In February 1956, Pan Am revised its Boeing order to just six JT3 models and 17 of the newly offered JT4-powered aircraft, to standardize the engines and get improved performance.

This transaction naturally attracted much attention from the other major airlines of the Western world. In October 1955, following the annual International Air Transport Association (IATA) meeting in New York, Douglas Sr. invited the top officials from 20 American and European airlines to visit his factory at Santa Monica where, on October 25, he and United President Pat Patterson jointly announced that

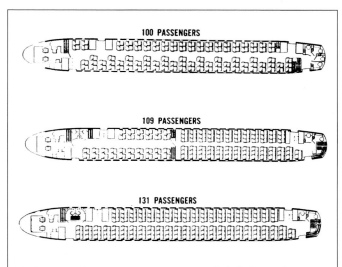

1955 proposed seating arrangements included: First-class (top); combination first- and tourist-class (middle); and all-tourist. Note the alternate four- and five-abreast layout in the top example.

United had ordered 30 DC-8s at a cost of $175 million, the largest single order ever placed for commercial airliners. Deliveries were scheduled to begin in May 1959.

National Airlines had leaked its intent to place an order for six DC-8s as far back as August 1955, but this was denied by Douglas until the formal signing on November 7. The first foreign buyer was an old Douglas customer, KLM, which purchased eight DC-8s on November 16, keeping intact its tradition of buying every Douglas airliner type since the DC-2 in 1934.

December saw a flurry of orders coming in. Eastern Air Lines President Eddie Rickenbacker announced a $165-million buy of 26 airplanes. The purchase consisted of a firm commitment for six Domestic versions, with initial deliveries in May 1959, followed by another 12, powered by "a much larger P&W engine," starting in March 1960. The last eight, on option, would be delivered commencing in the summer of 1961.

Next in line was Japan Air Lines, which, on December 15, announced a four-plane order for use on the Tokyo-Hawaii-San Francisco route; initial deliveries would begin in September 1960. Finally, on December 21, Scandinavian Airlines System (SAS), purchased seven firm plus three options, with deliveries slated to begin during the first quarter of 1960. Another customer was added without affecting the total sales when, on December 29, it was announced that four of Pan American's order would be allocated to Pan American-Grace (Panagra). By the end of 1955, Douglas had booked a total of 99 DC-8s from eight customers.

The Design Develops

Commensurate with all the sales activity, detail development began to pick up speed. Extensive laboratory testing began on hydraulics, electric and pressurization systems. Flight control system rigs were built, and cabin noise-level reduction was given a great deal of attention.

With the decision to have the engines mounted on pylons below the wing, there was great concern that the intakes

Blowaway jet (black arrows) disrupts vortices caused by the intake.

would act as vacuum cleaners, sucking in loose stones and debris while the power plants were being run up or during the initial takeoff roll. A similar problem was being experienced with the U.S. Air Force's B-66s. The feasibility of using a wire screen in the intakes was quickly discarded as such an installation would be subject to ice build-up. After extensive

study and testing, the problem was identified as a vortex which made itself apparent just forward and below the intake.

A Douglas aerodynamic engineer named Harold Klein solved the problem by directing a small amount of engine bleed-air at the base of the vortex to eliminate it. A squadron of B-66s was quickly modified for testing, and this addition proved to be a great success. It was to become known as the "blowaway jet" in Douglas sales brochures and was incorporated on the DC-8 pods.

To permit ground maneuvers in a restricted space, the main landing gear was re-designed. A two-by-two tandem wheel arrangement replaced the traditional single-coaxial layout. A great deal of effort and money was spent to design the bogie so that once the nose gear turned more than 45 degrees, the rear wheels of the inboard bogie unlocked and were free to castor, thus reducing the turning circle to a 91-foot radius at the wing tip. The wheels required a much smaller radius – only 29 feet – allowing easy 180-degree turns on runways. Tire wear due to scrubbing was also reduced considerably. Landing gear development alone exceeded the total cost of developing the DC-3.

A major concern was slowing the aircraft down because thrust-reversers had not yet been developed. Douglas addressed this by installing fighter-type air brakes just aft of the wing trailing-edge on the lower sector of the fuselage which could be deployed to make rapid descents or reduce roll-out on landing.

Noise was another problem that had to be tackled. Sixty acoustical, aerodynamics, and power plant engineers were assigned to the task. After considering over a thousand approaches to the problem and testing many scale models, a solution was reached, based on a Rolls-Royce design. The answer was a daisy-shaped exhaust section with eight petals, which reduced the noise by 10 decibels with minimal effect on performance.

While all this effort was in progress, several other major decisions were being made. By February 1956, the basic size of the DC-8 had grown considerably. Its wing span had increased to 139 feet, 9 inches, with a 5-foot extension incorporated at the root which added 160 square feet to the wing area. The fuselage had stretched by another 100 inches to an overall length of 148 feet, 10 inches, allowing seating for an additional 19 passengers in the economy configuration, still at the 40-inch seat pitch. Before the first flight, the length increased again, to 150 feet, 6 inches, due to re-design of the radome. The wing change was significant because it increased the fuel capacity by 20,000 pounds. Takeoff weights increased to 265,000 pounds for the Domestic version and 287,500 pounds for the Overwater version. The difference between the two models was still minimal, including some variations in skin thickness, structure modifications for the extra tankage and heavier landing gear in the long-range aircraft.

A "first" in the emerging jetliner industry was the Douglas decision to order a flight simulator for the DC-8 and have it operational before the airplane's maiden flight. On April 20, 1956, Douglas announced that it had contracted with Link Aviation Inc. to build a flight simulator to be located between the Santa Monica and Long Beach facilities.

Douglas DC-8 Specifications

DATA APPLICABLE TO ALL MODELS

Wing Area	2758 sq. ft.
Wing Span	139' 9"
Overall Length	148' 10"
Overall Height	42' 4"
Wing Sweepback (@ 25% Chord)	30°
Landing Gear Type (Swivel Caster)	Dual Tandem
Turning Radius (for wing tip clearance)	91' 1"
Lower Cargo Compartments (2)	
Total Volume—Both Compartments	1445 cu. ft.

*DATA APPLICABLE TO SPECIFIC MODELS LISTED

		Domestic First Class	Domestic First Class	Intercontinental (Mixed 1st Class-Tourist)	Intercontinental
Engines		JT3c-4 (J-57)	JT4A-3 (J-75)	**JT4A-3 **(J-75)	Conway
Design Gross Weight	lbs.	265,000	265,000	287,500	287,500
Max. Usable T. O. Weight	lbs.	250,000	265,000	287,500	287,500
Design Landing Weight	lbs.	189,000	189,000	190,500	190,500
Manufacturer's Weight Empty	lbs.	114,489	118,265	120,737	115,877
Operating Weight Empty	lbs.	119,726	123,532	128,862	123,726
Design Zero Fuel Weight	lbs.	161,200	165,000	167,550	163,750
Fuel Capacity	lbs.	114,400	114,400	140,500	140,500
Fuel Capacity	gals.	17,600	17,600	21,615	21,615
Capacity Payload (Space Limited)	lbs.	34,280	34,280	35,930	35,930
Number of Passengers		122	122	132	132
Cargo	lbs.	14,150	14,150	14,150	14,150
Range	st. mi.	3,550	4,030	4,470	4,810
Reserve Fuel	lbs.	16,500	16,680	17,180	16,800
Cost per Airplane Mile	$ st. mi.	1.54	1.72	1.93	1.835
Cost per Seat Mile	c seat mi.	1.26	1.41	1.46	1.39
Level Flight Speed Max. Cruise Thrust					
(a) at 30,000 ft., at 220,000 lbs	MPH T. A. S.	561	586	586	582
(b) at 30,000 ft., at 200,000 lbs	MPH T. A. S.	568	—	—	—
CAA Field Length Req'd for T. O. at Max. T. O. Weight	ft.	9,440	8,640	8,760	9,000
CAA Field Length Req'd for Ldg. at Max. Ldg. Weight	ft.	6,680	6,630	6,690	6,690
Range with 6500 ft. T. O. Field Length	(st. mi.)	1,830	2,650	3,060	3,280
TOURIST VERSION					
Capacity Payload Space Limited	lbs.	37,910	37,910	37,910	37,910
Number of Passengers		144	144	144	144
Cargo	lbs.	14,150	14,150	14,150	14,150
Range	st. mi.	3,290	3,790	4,330	4,670
Cost per Seat Mile	c	1.07	1.19	1.34	1.27
Range with 6500 ft. T. O. Field Length	(st. mi.)	1,770	2,495	2,960	3,190

* All range and performance data pertains to specific payload and weights indicated.
** Advanced rating.

February 1956

Simulators were not new, but this model would be much more realistic and sophisticated. Named Telerama, it used a television camera, traveling along tracks over an accurate scale model of an airfield to re-create the view from the cockpit. This forward-thinking paid off when, prior to the maiden flight, the test crew was able to log more than 35 hours training in the new simulator.

Several of the initial airline customers also placed orders for the simulator at the same time. It was felt important to have one available to the airlines as soon as possible to offset the cost of actual flight hours for training. Coincidentally, a proposal was being considered which would amend Civil Air Regulations to allow the use of simulators in lieu of aircraft for semi-annual pilot proficiency checks.

Yet another DC-8 model was introduced in May 1956,

when Trans-Canada became the 10th customer by ordering four Rolls-Royce Conway-powered versions at a cost of $5.5 million each. Earlier, Swissair had signed for three Overwater versions on January 30, followed by Delta's purchase of eight Domestic aircraft on February 13. Also in February, it was announced that Pan American had agreed to transfer four of its order to Panair do Brazil. After that initial rush, there was a gap of several months until November 19, when Union Aéromaritime de Transports (UAT) signed up for two Overwater versions at a unit price of $4.75 million. Shortly afterward, a second independent French airline, Transports Aériens Intercontinentaux (TAI) ordered four similar aircraft on December 20, bringing the sales total to 122 for 13 airlines. On October 1, 1963, these latest two customers merged to form Union des Transports Aériens (UTA).

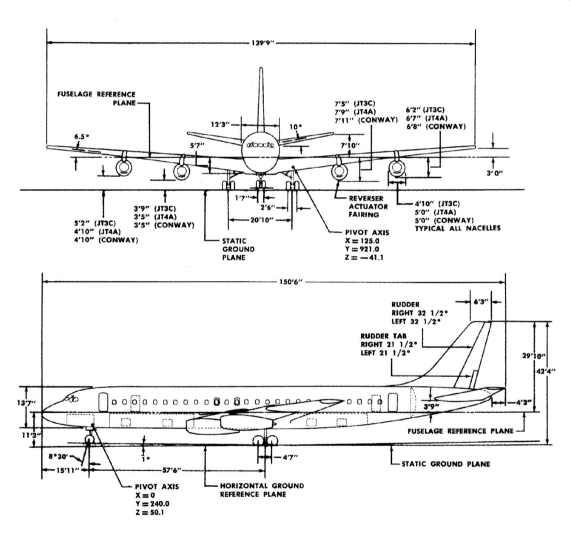

1958 Two-View Drawing

Wing Area	2,758 square feet
Wing Sweepback at 25 Per Cent Chord	30 degrees
Vertical Tail Area	352 square feet
Vertical Tail Sweepback at 25 Per Cent Chord	35 degrees
Horizontal Tail Area	559 square feet
Horizontal Tail Sweepback at 25 Per Cent Chord	35 degrees
Center of Gravity Limits	16.5 and 32 per cent MAC

CHAPTER II

Manufacturing The DC-8

Ship One's 19,000-pound fuselage being mated with the wings.

In June 1956, it was announced that an entirely new assembly building for DC-8 production would be erected on a 55-acre site adjacent to the existing Douglas facility at Long Beach, where two types of military aircraft, the C-133 "Cargomaster" turbo-prop transport and B-66/RB-66 "Destroyer" jet reconnaissance bomber were in production. The Long Beach factory, first opened in 1941, produced 4,285 C-47 variants and 3,000 Boeing B-17s for the war effort.

The new $20-million building consisted of two production halls, linked by a central core of offices, and covered a grand total of 1.14 million square feet, over 26 acres. The west hall – 1,144 feet long, 480 feet wide and 57 feet high – was for major sub-assembly fabrication of wings, fuselage barrels, cockpits, etc. It contained three bays spanning 160 feet each. The east hall was the same length, but 67 feet high, with two bays, 160 feet and 200 feet wide, respectively, accommodating a 12-position assembly line. After the aircraft passed the sixth position, it was taken outside where the fuselage was pressure-tested to 12.33 psi, then returned the assembly line. Target date for building completion was May 1957. In addition, a separate facility was erected nearby for aircraft exterior painting.

The Sheridan stretch former in action.

Douglas developed several innovative machines to facilitate DC-8 production. Foremost was the four-way stretch press, used to form the wing skins, a very complex operation. Douglas came up with the design parameters, then signed a contract with Sheridan-Grey Co. of Torrance, California to design and build it. Construction was completed in a record time of four months, at a cost of over $500,000. Weighing 720,000 pounds, it had four jaws, each capable of exerting 300 tons of pull. To hold the wing skin in place, a pressure of 2,400 tons was applied.

The wing panels were made from 75ST aluminum measuring 46 feet, 3 inches by 10 feet, 4 inches. Thickness tapered from 0.23 inches to 0.129 inches and each weighed 1,250 pounds. Manufactured by Aluminum Company of America (ALCOA) in Davenport, Iowa, the panels were shipped to Long Beach by rail, packed in dry ice, then stored in an adjacent freezer box (48 feet by 12 feet by 5 feet) until formed. This was to delay aging of the heat-treated panels until after stretching. Before being loaded onto the press, the correct panel shape was cut out using a full-size template and high-speed carbon-tipped cutters.

After forming, the skins were moved by an overhead crane system using vacuum pads to a 50-foot-long oven, placed on racks and heated to age the metal. Other specialized machines were used for the first time, including automatic drilling and riveting machines to fasten stringers to the wing skin. Similar devices were also used on the fuselage skin. Wing spars were milled on a U.S. government-owned Farnham machine already at Long Beach, leased by Douglas on an hourly basis. The first DC-8 spar cap was milled in September 1956, traditionally the first major component produced. Many other facilities and machines were rented via similar arrangements.

Re-allocation of manpower was in place to staff the new facility by early 1957. To ensure a production flow similar to that at the Santa Monica plant, many key personnel were assigned to the program. Heading the production department was D.H. Voss, a 23-year Douglas veteran who had been the superintendent of DC-6/7 sub-assemblies. Others who came were the former heads of planning, manufacturing control, production control and inspection. Overall responsibility was held by K.G. Farrar, vice president and general manager of the Long Beach Division.

Workers moved into the newly completed sub-assembly area of the plant on February 18, 1957, and started to erect the first cockpit section jigs. The official dedication ceremonies came on schedule May 10, when the second hall was completed. By October 25, 1957, the first wing-to-fuselage mating had taken place in the new building. It is worth recalling here that the entire airframe was built in-house; sub-contracting of major components was a rare event in those days. Eventually, Douglas did contract out the horizontal stabilizers to North American and engine pods were manufactured by Ryan in San Diego. However, hundreds of vendors, located throughout the United States, supplied specialized equipment and machined parts to Douglas.

Preliminary Test Program

Meanwhile, a huge water tank was fabricated at Long Beach to investigate the onset of metal fatigue caused by the effects of repeated cabin pressurization cycling, a direct cause of the early de Havilland Comet accidents. Investigation was carried out by the Royal Aircraft Establishment at Farnborough, England, where a water tank was used for the first time to investigate structural failure.

A 50-foot long fuselage section, including the cockpit because of the large number of skin cutouts, was installed in the tank, which contained hydraulic loading devices designed to function under water. With the fuselage cantilevered from a mocked-up center body section to simulate realistic support aft of the rear spar, the specimen and tank were filled with water simultaneously, precipitating a neutral pressure on the fuselage structure.

Through realistic and complex simulations, loading cycles were created to represent a takeoff, cruise and landing. These loads simulated cabin pressure, external aerodynamic forces and suctions, landing gear loads, etc. In the cruise portion, gust loads created by abnormal turbulence were introduced at more frequent intervals than would be experienced during normal flight operations. Even the loading and unloading of passengers and cargo was recreated.

A major design decision taken on the DC-8 was to introduce titanium strips as "rip stoppers" on the fuselage frames and around all skin cut-outs, such as windows and doors. (Use of substantial amount of titanium in the DC-8 was a first in commercial aircraft construction, and produced weight-savings of 500 pounds compared to conventional materials.) Almost 53,000 cycles were completed before any sign of repair work was needed. The first crack in an aluminum window frame appeared after over 113,000 cycles, but the titanium strap held. When cracks finally developed around the

The tape-controlled automatic drilling and riveting machine attaches stringers to a wing panel.

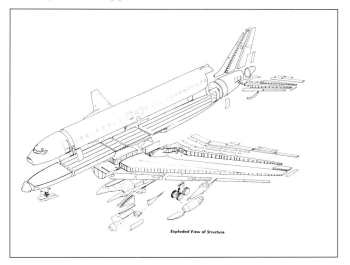

Exploded View of Structure

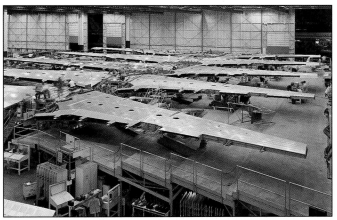

The author started his association with the DC-8 in 1968, as a liason engineer in this wing assembly area.

A double exposure shows the upward wing deflection on Ship Two during static tests.

windows, they were restricted to the outer skin, thus easily detected.

By the time of the DC-8's first flight, some 120,000 pressurization cycles had been completed. The program was terminated after the equivalent of 140,000 flights. A Douglas engineer at the time made a very prophetic statement: "The very low damage propagation rate after high-time exposure indicates that there will be no rapid deterioration of structure as the DC-8s become old." Almost 40 years later, his point has been well proven.

A second DC-8 cockpit section was shipped to the Civil Aeronautics Administration (CAA) Technical Development Center in Minneapolis to check out windshield resistance to bird strikes. The window pillars were made of steel, and windows consisted of two laminated panes, each capable of carrying the design loads. A layer of vinyl was added for impact strength and electrical heat was used to prevent fogging. The CAA regulations stipulated that cockpit windshields should withstand a direct bird strike at 391 mph, so a series of 4-pound chicken carcasses were fired at velocities up to 460 mph, with no significant damage to the windshields.

In another test, a section of fuselage was sealed and pressurized to represent the pressure differential at cruising altitudes. Steel harpoons were then used to penetrate the surface, in an attempt to cause an explosive decompression. But the titanium rip stops limited the size of the puncture to a small hole which allowed pressure to leak out slowly with no further damage.

Upon reaching structural completion, the second production aircraft was taken from the line and installed in a test rig. Lifting loads were applied to the wings via series of jacks working through a system of cables and beams erected above. Weights were installed in the fuselage; hydraulic struts simulated the engine loads; and the fuel tanks were pressurized.

Eventually, a maximum load of 462,012 pounds was applied to the wings which deflected the tips upwards over 67 inches. Downward loads were also applied, bending the tips down in excess of three feet from

Supplemental oxygen, reading lights, and air vents were contained in the Palomar seat backs. A first-class seat pair is shown.

Mock-up of a proposed five-abreast interior for SAS, circa 1959 .

the static position. The load was several times what could be expected in flight. No permanent wing distortion was detected through the myriad of strain gauges attached to the structure. After completion of the tests, Ship Two was returned to the production line for completion.

The Cabin Interior

Douglas had more experience than any other manufacturer when it came to designing cabin interiors. The company's well-established team was led by Jack Graves, who had been designing interiors since the DC-4. Traditionally, each was customized for the customer, so it was important to come up with as much layout flexibility as possible.

Many new concepts had to be created to accommodate this first-time use of six-across seating, which seriously affected the hat-rack design. (Closed bins were very much in the future.) The location of passenger service items such as lighting, oxygen masks and reading lights had to be reconsidered as well. In addition, it had to be a configuration that could be changed quickly from an all first-class (not unusual in those days) to a mixed class or high-density interior. Provision was made for 16 single-occupant upper berths to be made up during flight for first-class passengers. Moveable bulkheads were engineered to permit quick interior configuration changes to match route requirements.

Douglas engineers elected to create a new seat which integrated all the traditional passenger service items as well as folding seat-back trays. Fluorescent reading lights were mounted in the headrest, above and behind the passenger's shoulder. Emergency oxygen generated by a chemical pack was stowed in the seat back which also contained the oxygen mask. Incorporated in the same unit was an individual

First-class seating capacity on the early jets was nearly double that of even today's wide-body examples.

United's galley represented a typical layout. (United Airlines)

adjustable fresh air outlet and attendant call button. The outboard armrest ran the full length of the cabin, allowing easy relocation of the seat pitch as it incorporated plug-in connections for service items. The seat was unique in that it was attached to the side-wall and mounted on a single track in the floor. Patented by Douglas, the seat was named the "Palomar unitized seat" and used by all the customers until the introduction of the DC-8 Series 50CF. Interestingly, Douglas also used the name "Skyloge" when describing the seat. Four Douglas engineers shared a 1959 Industrial Designers Institute award recognizing the excellence of the seat design – the first time anyone in aviation had been so honored.

The lavatories and toilets were the subject of much design effort. For the first time, electro-mechanical flushing toilets were installed, a big improvement over the previous chemical variety. To provide hot water in the hand basins, a flash heater was located under the sink, with a single line coming from a cold water tank. Previously, two separate tanks were used, with an immersion heater providing hot water.

Interior noise suppression in the cabin was tackled in a new $250,000 acoustics laboratory, a first in the aircraft industry. A mock-up with a detailed cabin interior was located in a specially designed listening room, where high-fidelity reproductions of aircraft sounds were played back to verify cabin noise reduction methods and materials.

A 19,000-cubic foot anechoic (echoless) chamber was also used to analyze sound radiation from turbines, compressors, pumps and other internal equipment. The effect of metal fatigue caused by noise was explored separately in a special chamber.

A team of industrial designers worked with the airlines to develop custom decorative styles, including lighting, window coverings (which were all curtains), seat covers, and sidewall and bulkhead artwork. Other members of the team were involved with cabin crew representatives; designing galleys and developing meal service routines that were tried out in the mock-up.

DOUGLAS

Chapter III

Flight Testing

Roll-Out

O rders began to slow down as fewer airlines remained to be signed by either Douglas or Boeing. Olympic Airways ordered two JT4 versions on July 15, 1957, but these were quietly canceled by Douglas a year later because the airline was in danger of going out of business due to financial problems. However, United boosted the Douglas backlog on November 25 with an additional order for 10 aircraft. Trans-Caribbean Airways signed up for a single DC-8 on January 13, 1958, but later canceled it. The forfeited deposit was eventually applied to the purchase of a DC-8-50.

Alitalia followed on March 6, selecting four Rolls-Royce Conway models. Next was Iberia, coming in for two JT3-powered Overwater versions in May. It was apparent from these orders that Douglas was more interested in the longer-range markets, leaving the short-medium arena to the Boeing

720 and Convair 880. At this stage, Douglas sales were still lagging behind Boeing, but the gap was reasonably close with orders for 133 versus 150; not bad, considering the later start and the U.S.-government tanker order that allowed Boeing to be more price competitive.

On the final assembly line, more and more components were coming together, and by early spring 1958, the first 12 DC-8s were beyond the wing/fuselage mating phase. On March 28, the four Pratt & Whitney JT3s were attached to the pylons on Ship One.

The ambitious first flight date of December 1957, predicted back in 1955 by Douglas Sr., continued to slip. At one point, it was set for March 1958, but continued delays plagued the program. This was not a major surprise as the originally envisioned aircraft had passed through many design changes and grown because of customer demands. A lot of new ground was being explored and, to make up for lost

Photos show the ejector stowed (left) and deployed (right). The daisy-shaped silencer helped to reduce engine noise levels.

time, it was announced that a ninth aircraft would be added to the flight test program.

The 1957 Annual Report issued in April 1958 stated that the company had a total back-log order worth over $1.5 billion, including both commercial and military aircraft plus missile sales. The El Segundo division was busy building the F-4D Skyray, the Navy's A3D attack-bomber and the A4D Skyhawk. The C-133 was now in production at Long Beach, and Santa Monica was turning out the DC-6s and DC-7s.

In spite of the huge order book, cash flow associated with the DC-8 venture became a major concern to management. Over $200 million had already been invested, roughly equivalent to the company's net worth at the time. Over $90 million had been spent on research and development alone.

Traditionally, manufacturers have to borrow money and reinvest profits like any other business. Customer airlines usually would make a deposit of perhaps 25 percent of the purchase price, followed by a series of progress payments, bringing the total to 50 percent at delivery, when the balance would be paid in full. But this cash flow was not enough, and Douglas was forced to raise $60 million in debentures to cover part of its burgeoning expenditures. The extended design gestation period did not help the situation, and the break-even point was becoming more elusive. Art Raymond once stated, when the venture was first conceived in 1953, that the total market for commercial DC-8s was thought to be around 200, thus the expected break-even number must have been something less.

Eleven months after the new assembly hall was dedicated, Ship One (as the first aircraft was always referred to) ceremoniously "rolled out" on April 9, 1958. Waving from the open cockpit windows were Donald W. Douglas, Sr. and his son, Don Jr., by then president of Douglas Aircraft Company. Also in attendance were representatives of the 17 airline customers, including stewardesses from each carrier.

During the roll-out ceremonies, it was announced that a new sound suppressor, which incorporated a reverse-thrust system, had been designed by Douglas and would be added to production aircraft as soon as possible. It consisted of a sleeve, called an ejector, which slid aft for takeoff and landing, in effect extending the exhaust pipe, yet still allowing ambient air to mix with the exhaust gases. Also, two

Ship One (msn 45252) with two of its predecessors.

Ship One lifts off on its maiden flight.

clamshell doors, which lay flush when not in use, could be swung into the exhaust stream to re-direct the thrust forward during the landing roll. The unit also led to a slightly deeper pylon.

This system could be installed on both Pratt & Whitney engines as well as the Conway. Development costs for the new design, which reduced noise by another 10 decibels, exceeded $21 million.

First Flight

On May 30, 1958, before an estimated 95,000 employees and other onlookers, Ship One, registered N8008D, lifted off for the first time. Rotating at 128 knots after a ground roll of 3,250 feet, its JT3C engines left a trail of dense black smoke behind. Flown by a crew of three experienced test pilots, the DC-8 was airborne for 2 hours, 7 minutes, mainly over the Pacific Ocean, performing scheduled shakedown maneuvers before landing at Edwards Air Force Base (AFB). Takeoff weight was 198,000 pounds, and a speed of 350 knots at 21,000 feet was achieved during the flight, reported as an overwhelming success. Accompanying the aircraft as chase plane was a Cessna T-37 trainer and a United Air Lines DC-7 which carried the photographers.

The flight crew consisted of Heimie Heimerdinger as chief pilot, William "Bill" Magruder as co-pilot and Paul Patton at the flight engineer's station. Magruder subsequently went on to head the Federal Aviation Administration (FAA). Also on board was flight-test engineer Bob Rizer for

the purpose of monitoring the flight-data recorders mounted in the main cabin. Just aft of the forward-entry door, an escape chute and hatch were installed in the lower fuselage in case of rapid evacuation by parachute became necessary.

Early in the test program, a metal dummy of human weight was dropped through the escape chute, which extended into the slipstream after de-pressurization, to ensure that a safe bale-out could be accomplished. Although the dummy cleared the aircraft safely, its parachute failed to deploy automatically.

The second flight took place on June 4, when a 2-hour-5-minute flight was made from Edwards, followed by a 2-hour-40-minute flight on June 7. By the end of July, Ship One had flown 13 times and logged more than 45 hours in the air at speeds up to Mach 0.85, its design cruising speed at the intended long-range cruise altitude of 36,000 feet. Maximum takeoff weight with full fuel loads, was 255,000 pounds. Ship One returned to Long Beach on August 22 for a scheduled

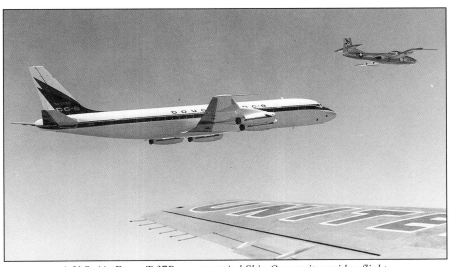

A U.S. Air Force T-37B accompanied Ship One on its maiden flight.

Ship One, shortly after arrival at Edwards Air Force Base, California, following a flawless first flight.

inspection and the installation of additional test equipment. By then, it had logged over 72 hours during 23 flights. Seven pilots had flown the aircraft, and all indicated that the handling was excellent.

The fuselage-mounted air brakes were eliminated early in the flight-test program, after the reverse-thrust system proved to be an excellent braking device. The air brakes were not very effective, and Douglas Chief Test Pilot Arnold G. "Heimie" Heimerdinger once stated, "Using them was like throwing out a couple of Kleenex tissues." Only Ships One and Two were flown with them installed.

Meanwhile, Douglas announced that the Overwater DC-8 performance would be improved yet again. Both the JT4 and Conway versions were to be offered with the takeoff weight being raised from 287,500 to 310,000 pounds. This increase allowed an additional 1,692 gallons of fuel to be carried with no reduction in payload. Several of the existing customers opted for the change. At the same time, recognizing that unscheduled down time would be costly to the airline, Douglas announced that it would to establish spare parts warehouses in New York and Europe.

The next three DC-8s to join the test fleet were all destined for United. A long interval between Ship One's maiden

First flight test crew Bill Magruder, Heimie Heimerdinger and Paul Patten.

flight and the next two first flights was created by the completion of static-testing on Ship Two, which made its maiden flight on November 29. Powered by JT4-9s, it bore the test registration N8018D and was in Douglas house colors. In an effort to explore performance improvements, the aircraft had 80-inch leading edge slots located between the fuselage and inboard pylons. For the initial flights, the slots were covered by temporary skin panels which could be removed later. After its initial flight trials, this aircraft was assigned to flutter investigation as well as pitch control and rejected takeoffs. Wing tufting was also added to check airflow distribution.

The third DC-8, N8028D, was late entering the test program due to installation of the new silencer and reverse-thrust systems. Equipped with JT3C-6 engines and used to check the fuel systems, flight controls and calibration, it first flew on December 28, in United's colors. All subsequent aircraft were built with the new engine systems. The initial three aircraft were based at Edwards AFB for the first six months; all other DC-8s remained at Long Beach for the test program.

Douglas failed to meet its goal of having four DC-8s flying in 1958. Ship Four, assigned test registration N8038D, made its initial flight in Douglas house colors on January 2, 1959, and was used to check out anti-icing systems, cabin pressurization and interior noise levels. The first flight by an FAA pilot, the formal start of certification, took place on January 29.

The first JT4-12-powered DC-8, N800PA, joined the test program on February 20, wearing Pan American Airways colors. A big advantage of the JT4 engine over the JT3, in addition to its increased power, was elimination of water-injection needed to improve takeoff performance. Distilled water, mixed with alcohol, provided denser air for better combustion. In addition, water's cooling effect allowed more fuel to be injected without exceeding the turbine-inlet temperature limits. However, it was a costly solution, requiring four 190-gallon tanks to feed the engines during takeoff. In all, 5,000 pounds of water was used for each departure! It greatly affected training flights because sufficient water was carried for only one takeoff.

Aside from further testing of the JT4s, N800PA was used to evaluate passenger boarding, cargo loading and the

First United DC-8-11 (line number 3/manufacturers serial number 45279) in full colors. It became N8002U in service.

Pan Am's DC-8-32, N800PA (ln 5/msn 45253) was the first to fly in airline colors. Bands on the starboard wing were for airflow testing.

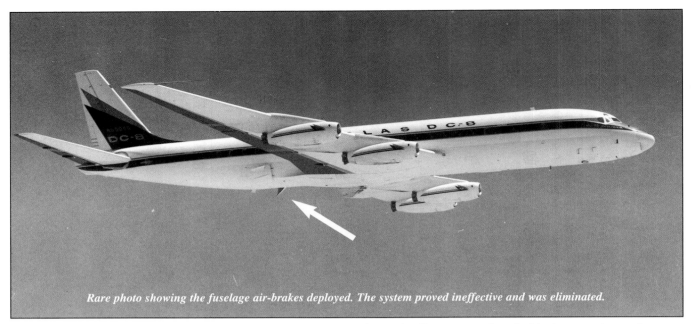

Rare photo showing the fuselage air-brakes deployed. The system proved ineffective and was eliminated.

hydraulic brake system. Two more DC-8s destined for Pan Am joined the test fleet for airport ground handling experience and noise monitoring checks. The first Rolls-Royce Conway-powered model (Ship Nine), temporarily registered N6577C, first flew on July 23, 1959.

An unusual incident took place on May 14 at Edwards AFB when, during trials to establish maximum allowable sink rates, Ship Two made a very hard landing resulting in the port outboard engine snapping off and striking the inboard engine. The engine pods were designed to break cleanly away under specific loading to prevent rupture of the fuel tanks in a wheels-up landing. In this case, the main damage was to the fuselage which buckled just aft of the wing trailing edge and sagged to the ground; the landing gear remained intact. FAA DC-8 Project pilot, Joe Tymczyszyn, who was in the left seat, and Heimerdinger brought the aircraft to a safe stop after turning onto a taxiway. The pilots only realized the extent of the damage after shutting down the systems, and going aft to attend to flight-test engineer Bill Bryde, who was slightly injured. Subsequent examination revealed no damage to the wing or landing gear, and no fuel leaks were detected.

Douglas engineers had predicted that a sink rate of 1,500 feet per minute (fpm) would be achievable, but as the pilots thought this was too high, it was decided to start the trials at a sink rate of 1,000 fpm and work up in increments. Several increases had already been successfully accomplished prior to an attempted landing at an 1,175-fpm sink rate. At the correct height of 51 feet, indicated by a sensor, power was retarded and a stick-back pressure of 118 pounds was applied to flare the aircraft. The nose pitched up, but the aircraft continued to descend at the same sink rate until the main gear struts were fully compressed and the rear fuselage snapped downwards. In the ensuing inquiry, the crew were absolved of all blame. Subsequently, the aircraft was repaired at Edwards and ferried to Long Beach. Part of the repair included strengthening the keel beam, a change incorporated on all production aircraft.

Before being handed over to United as N8001U in November 1960, Ship Two was re-certified as a model 21. After logging over 52,000 flight hours with United, it was

Ship Two, (ln 2/msn 45278) after its heavy landing at Edwards on May 14, 1959. (Base Historian, Edwards AFB)

Ship Four, N8038D (ln 4/msn 45280), a model 11, seen at the American Institute of Aeronautics & Astronautics (AIAA) meeting, at Las Vegas in 1960.

(Bob Archer)

traded to Boeing in January 1978 and later scrapped at Kingman, Arizona.

Another little-publicized event of great importance took place on September 22, 1959, when Patent No. 186,199 was awarded for the DC-8 basic design in the name of Chief Engineer Ed Burton. It had been applied for on April 25, 1956 and was good for 14 years from the date of issue.

As the flight test program accelerated, so did the DC-8. Speeds of Mach 0.98 were reached and the effects of compressibility were experienced above Mach 0.92. Stable cruise

Note the "DC8-DM/Ship 3/UAL" stenciled on the fuselage of N8028D (ln 3/msn 45279) for identification purposes prior to delivery.

Delta's first DC-8-11, N801E (ln 14/msn 45408), heads down the production line on May 13, 1959. The Delta airplane, Fuselage 14, was nearly complete even as the first DC-8 flight was still two weeks away.

could be flown at Mach 0.88. All the later models of the DC-8 were put into a dive to reach Mach 0.95 during certification trials. Flights were flown to 40,000 feet, then the cabin pressurization system was turned off to check for leaks. Peak cruise altitudes of 45,000 feet were also attained. Icing tests were flown with strips of wood applied to the leading edges to represent ice build-up, in addition to flights into actual icing conditions.

Center-of-gravity limits were confirmed by pumping water between two large tanks temporarily located fore and aft in the cabin. Low-frequency flutter was created by wingtip-mounted vane "exciters," to confirm damping out capabilities. By firing the equivalent of 12-gauge shotgun cartridges at the fin and stabilizer tips, high-frequency flutter oscillations were induced and measured by telemetry. During these trials, all the crew wore hard hats! Stall recovery was clean, with an altitude loss of only a few hundred feet. For these tests, a large drag-chute was fitted in the tail cone of Ship One to assist in recovery if problems arose. The 28-foot diameter chute was designed to reduce speed from 420 knots to 300 knots in 15 seconds. The first time deployment was attempted, the handle was pulled and nothing appeared to happen. A few seconds later, the chute deployed and the aircraft slowed as expected, giving the crew quite a jolt.

The intensive test program required 26 Douglas test pilots to be qualified on the DC-8. Only about half of them had any previous military jet experience. Don Mullin, for example, had flown only propeller-driven transports during his naval career before joining the company as a DC-6/DC-7 test pilot. At the other extreme, Bill Bridgeman had flown the

Douglas Skyrocket at Mach 1.40 and also the Douglas X-3 Stiletto. Each pilot spent 15 hours in the simulator before transitioning to the left seat of the DC-8. Airline pilots were also put through the training program and given the opportunity to share some of the routine flying.

After a DC-8 demonstrated that it could operate safely from Bogota Airport, Colombia, over 8,000 feet above sea-level, it was approved to operate into La Paz Airport, Bolivia, at an elevation of 13,355 feet. Once, over Mexico City, a fully loaded DC-8 demonstrated an emergency descent from 42,000 feet to 14,000 feet in 47 seconds without causing discomfort to the passengers.

On July 24, 1959, Ship Seven, a DC-8-32 destined to be Pan Am's N802PA, was assigned to route-proving and airline-flight schedules. Called "Operation Young Airlines," it was temporarily registered N8068D and painted in Douglas house colors while covering over 100,000 miles in a six-week period. Fifty-four flights were made to destinations such as Madrid and Montreal. A nonstop flight from Long Beach to London on September 3 covered the distance in a record-setting 10 hours, 42 minutes.

On February 4, 1960, Douglas Vice President of Commercial Programs Jackson R. McGowen announced the now familiar DC-8 model identification system. The first Domestic version with JT3C-6 engines was designated the DC-8 Series 10. Domestic aircraft with the follow-on JT4A power plants were to be known as the DC-8 Series 20. The Overwater model with JT4A engines were designated DC-8 Series 30, and the Conway-powered aircraft became the DC-8 Series 40.

In addition, the new DC-8 Series 50, fitted with Pratt & Whitney JT3D turbofans, was mentioned for the first time.

As the flight test program progressed, it became apparent that aircraft drag was higher at cruise speeds than had been predicted by wind-tunnel tests. At the time, Douglas had little experience in the correlation between wind tunnel data and actual flight performance in the high-Mach cruise range intended for the DC-8. Conflicting data from several different wind-tunnel models also contributed to the problem.

The guarantee was for a maximum cruise speed of 493 knots at 30,000 feet on an aircraft fitted with JT3C-6 engines and weighing 220,000 pounds, but only 469 knots was being achieved. Under the same conditions, the JT4A versions were within 2 knots of the guaranteed 511 knot speed. Ship Two was grounded for a series of wing modifications. A revised tip profile, added to reduce the effective wing sweep, increased the span to 142 feet, 4 inches. This change reduced the high speed drag, thus increasing both speed and range. Vortex generators were considered for the wing upper surfaces – Boeing's solution – but the DC-8 did not need them. Changes were also made to the size and shape of the engine exhaust cone.

The DC-8 handled well at the low end of the speed scale, but the pylon/wing intersection caused a great deal of drag. Cambering the pylons alleviated this to a degree, but created other problems with the wing's lift coefficient, so a system of wing leading-edge slots was installed, including the previously tried inboard 80-inch slot, plus a 32-inch example, located inboard of each outboard pylon. All were covered by flush-fitting doors which opened when the flaps were extended. This improved the slow-speed lift characteristics so much that the MTOW was increased by 8,000 pounds for the same field length requirements. Boeing and Convair had similar problems with their designs; Convair also added the leading-edge slots, while Boeing added leading-edge "barn door" flaps.

Typical leading edge slot with covers in the open position.

Despite these changes, the Series 30 model was not meeting its original range and performance guarantees. After much negotiation, including a substantial price reduction, the airlines agreed to take the aircraft. However, Donald Douglas, Sr., who built the company on his reputation for personal integrity, gave orders that the guarantees must be met, regardless of the cost.

During the flight test program, only three new customers purchased DC-8s. Northwest Orient Airlines ordered five Series 30s on December 30, 1958 followed by Philippine Airlines – closely allied to KLM – signing for two -30s in April 1959. The biggest order came in October, when Canadian Pacific made public its decision to purchase four DC-8s plus five options powered by Rolls-Royce Conway engines of 16,500 pounds thrust. Shortly thereafter, Rolls-Royce announced that the thrust rating of its Conway (RCo) 12 Mark 508 would be increased to 17,500 pounds. In addition, more follow-up orders had been taken. KLM firmed up four options, plus one from the previous buy, for five Series 50s to be powered by JT3D turbofan engines. Two other unidentified international airlines added a total of seven re-orders. Meanwhile, United had revised its planned fleet of 40 JT3C-6 powered aircraft to just 18, the balance of 22 being upgraded to Series 21s with a 310,000-pound MTOW, powered by the JT4A-3 engines of 15,800 pounds thrust.

Majestic in flight, Ship One cruises over the California high desert.

Chapter IV
Airline Operations

Guests inspect the first DC-8 to be delivered, United's model 11, N8004U (ln 8/msn 45281) on June 3, 1959.

The DC-8 Enters Service

First deliveries to an airline began on June 3, 1959, when Ship Eight, DC-8-11 N8004U, was delivered to United at a factory ceremony. With much fanfare, Donald Douglas, Sr. handed over the log books to Pat Patterson. This and the next five ships, delivered over the following three months, would be used for crew training. United planned to commence service with at least six aircraft in hand. Crew qualification was rapid, thanks to the airline's early purchase of a DC-8 flight simulator.

During United's crew training, a serious aircraft defect was revealed. The ground spoilers were designed to activate once the nose wheel had settled on the ground. During a touch-and-go landing at San Francisco Airport, the nose gear had just contacted the runway as the aircraft transgressed the slight rise of an intersecting runway. This created a pronounced longitudinal "porpoising" effect. As the nose gear compressed and extended, the spoilers extended and retracted, so the pilot manually retracted the spoilers and continued

the takeoff. This incident resulted in a change to the spoiler retract cycle. Later, another modification was introduced which extended the spoilers when the main gear started to rotate after touchdown.

Problems had also surfaced during earlier flight tests, owing to the insufficient size and poor location of the cockpit spoiler handle. In one rejected takeoff test at 185 knots, the co-pilot had trouble locating the handle, resulting in heavy braking which caused all eight tires to blow out as the aircraft ran off the end of the runway.

Delta took delivery of its first DC-8-11 on July 21 and, on the following day, set a 1-hour-28-minute speed record between Miami and Atlanta. Delta's second aircraft followed on September 14.

On August 25, as part of the FAA test program, a JT4A-powered aircraft made a 4,500-mile round-trip via airway routes from San Diego to Jacksonville, Florida. This was the last flight needed before the FAA would issue official approval for the DC-8 to begin carrying fare-paying passengers.

Pioneering slide photographer Dean Slaybaugh captured the first DC-8-11 (N801E, ln 14/msn 45408) for Delta outside the main assembly hall in June 1959.

member, Douglas had mounted the first officer's seat on extended tracks to permit the occupant to slide back and monitor the systems panel. When the DC-8 was being reviewed for Canadian use, that country's Department of Transport specified a three-person cockpit also, but was ambivalent as to whether the third crew member was a pilot or flight engineer. The DC-8 cockpit was very spacious, and Overwater aircraft were all also equipped with a navigator's station behind the captain's seat.

A big disappointment to Douglas and the airlines was the FAA's decision requiring the DC-8 to be flown by a crew of three pilots. Hoping to eliminate the need for third crew

Perhaps the most important flight that Ship Seven made as part of the "Young Airline" intensive flying program was a flight from Long Beach to Baltimore on August 31, 1959. On board were both Donald

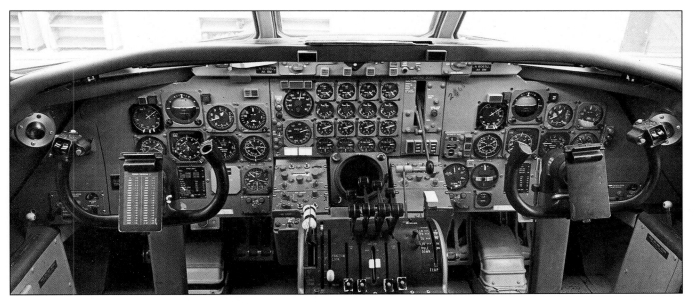

Top: *Cockpit of United DC-8-52, N8065U (ln 230/msn 45756).*
Lower left: *Mock-up of navigator's position for Overwater aircraft.* **Lower right:** *Flight Engineer's panel.*

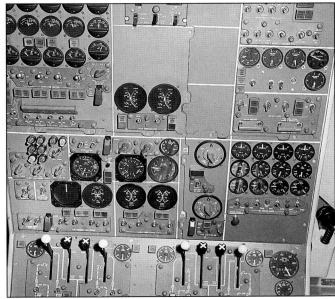

Douglas, Sr. and Jr. with key members of the DC-8 management team and a distinguished group of guests from the customer airlines. The purpose of the flight was to receive the FAA type certificate for the DC-8 Series 11, one month ahead of schedule. The flight test program had entailed 2,284 flight hours and 1,782 sorties, including over 1,300 hours of precisely controlled and instrument-monitored tests under all types of operating conditions.

The certificate was presented to Mr. Douglas at Baltimore's Friendship Airport by Elwood R. Quesada, chief administrator of the FAA. The following day, the party flew on to Idlewild Airport (now JFK) in New York for a major press conference which was also attended by Pat Patterson and Delta President C. E. Woolman. The DC-8-11, without a slotted wing, was certificated for a MTOW of 265,000 pounds and a maximum landing weight (MLW) of 190,500 pounds. At the time of certification, Douglas had received orders for 143 DC-8s from 18 airlines.

Service Start-up

September 18, 1959 became a banner day for the DC-8 when Delta Air Lines and United Air Lines both introduced DC-8s into revenue service. By reason of time zone differences, Delta beat United by a scant 2 hours, 10 minutes to become the first to put a DC-8 into airline operation. Its Flight 823 departed Idlewild for Atlanta at 9:20 a.m., while United left San Francisco bound for Idlewild at 8:30 a.m. local time, 11:30 a.m. in New York. Both airliners were in mixed dual-class configurations.

One point often overlooked with the introduction of jet aircraft was the impact on passenger ground handling. Until the advent of jetliners, the use of a covered "airbridge" or "jetway" was virtually unknown. Larger airlines such as Pan Am, United and Delta hustled to re-design existing terminals or build new ones to handle nose-in docking as a space-saver and ease passenger boarding. Delta's first airbridge at its Atlanta terminal became operational only a few hours before the first DC-8 arrived.

Although Douglas slipped behind its originally proposed in-service date, it had shortened the Boeing lead considerably. Forced into re-design of the fuselage – both in diameter and length – for the commercial market, Boeing encountered drag problems similar to those endured by Douglas. The 707 began scheduled service with Pan Am October 26, 1958, on the New York-London route, three weeks after BOAC started Comet 4 service over the same route. But the 707 did not start domestic service until National Airlines leased a Pan Am airplane for its New York-Miami service on December 10, 1958. American began transcontinental 707 flights January 25, 1959 between New York-Idlewild and Los Angeles.

During the rest of 1959, twenty-one DC-8s came off the production line, mainly for immediate delivery to either United or Delta. The only exception was Ship 18, a second DC-8-41 for TCA; it joined the test fleet as N6578C.

On January 3, 1960, Eastern Air Lines took delivery of the first DC-8 Series 21. Powered by the 15,800-pound thrust JT4A-3 and fitted with the slotted wing, its MTOW was 276,000 pounds, and MLW 199,500 pounds. Eastern had originally ordered Series 10s, but switched when the Series 20 became available sooner than expected. All production aircraft from Ship 30 onwards were manufactured with slots. A few were delayed pending slot installation, which saved necessary re-certification.

N8602 (ln 36/msn 45423), a DC-8-21 of Eastern, still displaying production line information on its nose-wheel door.
Inset: *Eastern Air Lines first-class lounge.*

The FAA issued a type certificate for the DC-8-21 on January 19, and Eastern initiated service between New York-Idlewild and Miami the following day. Within a month, Eastern had received three more DC-8s, and began advertising them as "DC-8Bs." In June, National and Delta filed complaints with the Civil Aeronautics Board (CAB), arguing that no such model existed. In October, the CAB ruled in Eastern's favor, recalling that Douglas had originally marketed DC-8A and DC-8B models based on engine installed, either the JT3 or JT4. Later, Pan American, Northwest and National were to go one better, and referred to their DC-8-32s as "DC-8Cs." However, in February 1961, after an appeal by Delta, and refusal by Douglas to formalize the DC-8A/B designations – and upset United – which was flying both models, Eastern was ordered to drop the designation and use the official DC-8-21 nomenclature instead.

Meanwhile, certification of the DC-8-30 and DC-8-40 series was being completed and, on February 1, 1960, the FAA issued type certificates for the DC-8-31 and DC-8-32 simultaneously. The -31 was approved for 300,000 pounds MTOW, and the -32 cleared for 310,000 pounds. Both models had JT4A-9s, rated at 16,800 pounds static thrust, plus the slotted wing and extended tips. However, the DC-8-32 also

had a modified flap linkage, which allowed the flaps to droop 1.5 degrees in cruise, significantly improving performance. In addition, the model 32 carried an additional 980 gallons of fuel in new leading-edge tanks. On March 23, the DC-8-41 received its type certificate and was also cleared to 300,000 pounds MTOW with the slotted wing and tip modifications incorporated.

National Airlines was the next customer to start DC-8 operations. Its first DC-8-21 was handed over on February 7, and entered service between New York and Miami four days later, on the 11th. A second aircraft was accepted on March 7. Until April 24, National held the distinction of being first to operate the DC-8 and B707 simultaneously. Later, Pan Am and Braniff, followed by several cargo and supplemental air carriers, had mixed fleets with both types.

Delayed by three to five weeks in order to add the slots and revised wing tips prior to delivery, Pan Am's first DC-8-32, N804PA, was handed over on February 7. The three others produced earlier were still in the flight-test program for further up-grading of performance and engines. Pan Am initiated DC-8 service between New York and Bermuda on March 27, and began flights to London a month later, on April 27.

Both of Canada's major airlines selected Rolls-Royce-powered DC-8-40s.
Above: DC-8-42 CF-TJF (ln 117/msn 45566) of Air Canada. (Author)
Below: DC-8-43 CF-CPJ (ln 183/msn 45661) in original Canadian Pacific colors.

TCA's CF-TJI (ln 127/msn 45611) crashed near Barbados in February 1976, while operating for Cubana as CU-T1210.

February 7 continued to be a big day at Long Beach as the first DC-8-41, CF-TJD, was handed over to Trans-Canada Airlines. A second followed immediately and, after some crew training, both flew to the new TCA Montreal maintenance base which was just being opened. DC-8 flights started between Montreal, Toronto and Vancouver on April 1. Trans-Atlantic service commenced June 1, between Toronto and London via Montreal.

By the end of February 1960, production had reached the scheduled rate of eight aircraft per month. Thirty DC-8s were in service, and assembly of Ship 100 had begun.

As part of Douglas Sr.'s promise to meet performance guarantees, a DC-8-11 was test flown on February 17, re-fitted with wing slots and extended wing tips. A short certification flight-test program resulted in a new type certificate, issued on July 1, for the DC-8-12 variant. The MTOW was increased from 265,000 to 273,000 pounds. Over time, both United and Delta modified their fleets to the model 12 standard; United subsequently upgraded its airplanes to the DC-8-21 specification.

As the flight test program wound down and the majority of the test aircraft were refurbished for delivery to the airlines, Ship One, N8008D, returned to Long Beach in March for conversion to the prototype DC-8 Series 50, equipped with JT3D turbo-fan engines.

KLM became the first European airline to accept a DC-8, on March 19, and initiated service between Amsterdam and New York on April 16, building its frequency level to a daily service 10 days later. Like KLM, SAS had chosen the model 32 and received its first on March 31, and introduced jet service between Copenhagen and New York on May 1. Alitalia accepted its first -42 on April 28 and commenced Rome-New York jet service June 1. Following an initial delivery on May 18, Northwest inaugurated trans-Pacific services on July 8 from Seattle to Tokyo and Manila via Anchorage.

Panagra's first DC-8-31 was accepted on April 6, 1960, and entered service between Buenos Aires and New York on May 2 via an interchange agreement. Panagra operated the DC-8 northbound as far as Panama, where a Pan Am crew took it on to Miami. The Miami-New York sector was flown by National crews. The same arrangement took place on the southbound services. In February 1967, Panagra merged with Braniff, which continued to operate both the aircraft and route.

The first DC-8-32 for KLM, PH-DCA (ln 48/msn 45376) flew for 10 different airlines before retiring in 1980.

Alitalia DC-8-42 I-DIWA (ln 57/msn 45598). Later converted to a model 43F, it crashed near Mexico City in August 1980 while owned by Aeronaves del Peru.

Panagra's DC-8-32 N8274H (ln52/msn 45274), spent most of its career with Capitol International as N905CL.

OY-KTA (ln 50/msn 45384) of SAS at Los Angeles in 1968. (Author)

Aeronaves de Mexico DC-8-21 XA-XAX (ln 105/msn 45432) was originally to be Eastern's N8611.

At the annual Douglas stockholders meeting in April, it was disclosed that the company had suffered nearly $7 million in losses during the first quarter, mostly attributed to heavier than expected DC-8 costs. The president stated, "In original planning for the DC-8, cost was expected to fall below the selling price at the 20th airplane. Cross-over is now expected at number 70." This situation prevented the planned launch of the DC-9 for 1960 as Douglas sought to reduce its borrowing costs by cutting its revolving credit line by 33 percent.

In July, as part of a training flight for TAI crews, a DC-8 took a Douglas sales team, led by Mr. Douglas, Sr., to Mexico City on a demonstration flight. The return journey, on July 27, established a speed record of 2 hours, 43 minutes for the 1,560-mile Mexico City-Los Angeles segment. The sales effort was considered successful when Aeronaves de Mexico (ADM) ordered two DC-8-50s. In the interim, a new DC-8-21, originally destined for Eastern, was bought off the production line by ADM and entered service in November 1960 as XA-XAX. However, it was written off at New York-Idlewild two months later, following an aborted takeoff.

In September 1960, it was announced that a modified leading edge, with a sharper nose and 4 percent chord increase from root to tip, was being developed to reduce drag at high Mach conditions.

In addition, the leading-edge slots were lengthened. The wing area increased from 2,773 to 2,868 square feet, allowing additional fuel cells in the new leading edge. The drag had been generated because the airfoil's blunt nose caused significant shock waves to appear at cruise conditions.

Testing confirmed a range increase of 8 percent, a speed increase of 0.02 Mach, and 7,000 pounds of additional payload. The revised leading edge was offered as a retrofit for any of the aircraft already built, and become standard from line number 148 onward. All Series 40s and 50s were approved to fly with the new leading edge on October 10, 1961. In addition, the DC-8-21 was re-certified on July 27, 1962 with the 4-percent-leading-edge addition, which allowed upgrading of some earlier models to DC-8-50 series standards. The price of the retrofit kit was less than $200,000 per aircraft.

Japan Air Lines, a major customer, accepted its first DC-8-32 on July 16, 1960, starting Tokyo-Honolulu-San Francisco service on August 12. TAI, the French independent airline, followed on September 4, flying between Paris and Nadi and Nadi-Los Angeles, connecting with the Air France service to Paris, thus providing around-the-world service. Union Aéromaritime de Transport (UAT), the other French independent carrier, began services between Paris and Brazzaville, French West Africa, on September 10, having received its first delivery on June 27. Earlier, in January, UAT had been having second thoughts about the DC-8 possibly

N803US (ln 84/msn 45604) was one of five DC-8-32s flown by Northwest Orient from 1960 to 1962.

Above: *JA8001 (ln 78/msn 45418), JAL's first DC-8-32, was retired in 1974 and used as a cabin trainer. The cockpit section still exists.*
Below: *DC-8-32 F-BJLA (ln 71/msn 45567) of UAT, later UTA. It was sold to Spanish carrier TAE for charter work in 1973, becoming EC-CDC.*

TAI DC-8-33 F-BJLA (ln 71/msn 45567) operated a series of sub-services on behalf of Air Madagascar in 1962. (Author's Collection)

being too big for its routes, and offered them for sale, hoping for the Comet 4C as a replacement. Initially, UAT had wanted to buy three DC-8s, but the French government would not approve more than two.

July 16 also saw the start of Northwest Orient's DC-8 flights, between New York and Seattle, but in October, the carrier's new jets were grounded for two weeks because of a strike by DC-8 flight engineers who were seeking higher pay for international flights. Another milestone occurred on October 11, when SAS inaugurated nonstop trans-polar DC-8 service from Copenhagen to Seattle.

An SAS DC-8 survived a near disaster during a night takeoff from Copenhagen in August 1960 when it ran into a huge flock of seagulls. Three engines and the leading edge were badly damaged. Due to heavy fog in northern Europe, the aircraft was forced to circle for four hours before landing. Two days later, it was back in service with new engines and leading edges installed.

Lack of performance, pending the introduction of the 4-percent-leading-edge modification, caused problems for several European airlines. Stronger winter winds forced trans-Atlantic westbound flights to stop for fuel, usually at Shannon or Gander. SAS, in conjunction with Swissair, set up a program to install an additional 950 gallons of fuel in the wing leading edges; the two carriers already had a pool agreement in place for spares and maintenance. Alitalia also added this extra tankage. KLM did not, but later added the 4 percent leading edge.

The remaining flight test work in 1960 included certification of the first three Pan Am aircraft to the DC-8-33 specification, which incorporated the revised tips and flap linkage, plus slotted wings and upgraded 17,500-pound thrust JT4A-11 engines. On November 28, the DC-8-33 received its type certificate, with a 315,000-pound MTOW.

Pan Am eventually upgraded its remaining -32s to -33s, during regular maintenance periods.

By the end of the year, 16 airlines had taken delivery of 111 DC-8s in eight different model variations, each airline having selected its own customized cockpit and interior. The total order book stood at 156 aircraft.

An interesting sideline to new sales has been the acceptance in trade of older aircraft as partial payment. The DC-8 program was no exception to this type of negotiation. For example, Douglas accepted 10 DC-7s from United and five

Varig DC-8-33 PP-PDS (ln 118/msn 45272), purchased from Panair do Brazil in July 1965, is seen at Paris-Orly.
(Author's Collection)

Operated by Air Ceylon in 1977, DC-8-43 4R-ACT (ln 42/msn 45445) was originally Air Canada's CF-TJD. (H. Oehninger)

Lockheed 1049D Super Constellations from TCA. These propliners, stored at Las Vegas to avoid California inventory taxes, were sold off, by R. James Pfeiffer and Associates on behalf of Douglas.

Meanwhile, airline customers requested the ability to ferry a spare engine to a distant location when required for a disabled aircraft. At the request of QANTAS, Boeing came up with an aluminum and plastic fairing, known as a "Pod Pak," to carry a pylon-mounted spare power plant inboard of the number 2 engine. Douglas designed a similar installation which was FAA-approved for the DC-8-21 and the Series 30 on December 5, 1960; the Series 40 installation was certified on May 2, 1961. It was designed to break down into 15 components for easy stowage in the cargo hold when not in use. Panair do Brazil was the first to make operational use of the pod in March 1961. This technique is still used today on most modern wide-body transports.

Three-engine ferry flights (without passengers) were also approved for the DC-8, beginning with the DC-8-11, on October 13, 1960; all remaining variants were certified by May 1961.

The first DC-8-43 was delivered to Canadian Pacific Airlines (CPA) on February 22, 1961 and entered service April 30 on a route from Amsterdam, via Canadian cities, to Auckland and Sydney. On May 31, CPA started nonstop Amsterdam-Vancouver polar flights, followed a week later by Japan Air Lines, with service between Tokyo and New York. Panair do Brazil received two DC-8s on March 21 and put them in service shortly afterward, between Buenos Aires and Frankfurt via Rio de Janeiro, plus a second service to Beirut, with several intermediate stops.

During June 1961, Delta set three DC-8 speed records: Atlanta-Los Angeles in 4 hours, 9 minutes; Los Angeles-Atlanta in 3 hours, 27 minutes; and Los Angeles-New Orleans also 3 hours 27 minutes.

In the first two years of operation, all the early jets had a number of teething problems with hydraulics, braking, control systems and landing gear failures. For example, an Eastern DC-8 drifted off the runway at Miami on July 12, 1961 after a hydraulic pump failed; there was no damage. On September 16, a Pan Am DC-8 en route to Bermuda suffered hydraulic problems in the air and returned to Idlewild, where the right main gear collapsed on touchdown. No serious injuries were reported, though both starboard engines became detached. In one week during October, two United DC-8s and a Western Airlines 720B made precautionary landings at Edwards Air Force Base and a Braniff 707 diverted to Carswell Air Force Base, all due to hydraulic failure indications.

This flurry of incidents caused the FAA to hold meetings with all the manufacturers in an attempt to improve the situation. Eastern's Air Line Pilot's Association (ALPA) Council said in a letter to the FAA that it would not allow its members to fly DC-8s unless the FAA reconfirmed the plane's airworthiness in writing. The FAA could find no consistency in the failures or any basic design faults, and concluded that the DC-8's hydraulic problems were no worse than any other type. However, all the manufacturers responded in a positive manner.

Douglas designed a number of improvements to the flap hydraulic systems, added additional fluid reservoirs and introduced various pressure-relief valves and a separate system for nose wheel steering. The FAA added more inspectors to monitor airline maintenance bases and ensure the correct use of parts. By December, most airlines were making the improvements at their own maintenance facilities during an average two-day down-time per aircraft. New

Air France operated DC-8-33 OO-TCP (ln 91/ msn 45265) during the summer of 1973. (Eric LeGendre)

Zambia Airways leased DC-8-43 9J-ABR (ln 73/msn 45599) from Alitalia for six years. It was eventually sold to IAS Cargo for spare parts, in 1976. (B. Stainer)

Air Jamaica's DC-8-43 6Y-JME (ln 9/msn 45442), one of several acquired from Air Canada. (Jeff Burch)

Formerly owned by Pan Am, DC-8-33 OO-TCP (ln 91/msn 45265) flew with short-lived Belgian charter operator Pomair for three years before joining Capitol International as N900CL. (Pol van Damme)

deliveries had the changes already incorporated. By April 1962, the FAA's goal to reduce the incident rate by 50 percent had been achieved.

The first DC-8 mechanical failure resulting in fatalities took place at Denver on July 11, 1961, when a United aircraft slewed off the runway after touchdown. The landing gear collapsed and a resulting fire destroyed the aircraft, killing 17 people. The cause was traced to a reverser bucket failing to lock as full-reverse thrust was applied, causing the aircraft to lose directional control. A new interlock was designed to prevent recurrence, either on the ground or in the air.

During this period, air safety had reached a crisis level, as 995 passengers and crew died during the first nine months of 1961, in 34 separate airliner crashes; 316 people were killed in September alone. However, it is worth noting that only four crashes involved jet airliners.

"Pod Pak" installation on a Garuda DC-8-55.

Production rates throughout the industry began to drop off during 1961 as new orders slowed down. The initial surge of jetliners entering service receded when airlines, absorbing the impact of expensive new aircraft funding, waited for traffic growth to catch up. Forty-three DC-8s were delivered to 12 airlines, including initial delivery to Panair do Brazil of a Series 30. First deliveries of Series 50s were made to Iberia, Trans-Caribbean, KLM and United.

In June 1961, United took delivery of the last model 12, and TAI accepted the last -33; the final DC-8-21 went to Eastern in October. Production then concentrated on the Series 40s and 50s. Alitalia established a new speed record November 6, when a DC-8-43 on delivery made the trip from Long Beach to Rome in 10 hours, 43 minutes, reaching ground speeds as high as 691 mph.

Repeat orders for DC-8-50s trickled in from Delta, KLM, JAL, National, United and Trans Caribbean and a new customer, Venezolana Internacional De Aviación, S.A. (VIASA), which ordered two Series 50s in April. Typical of aircraft pricing at that time, Interavia Airletter reported that JAL's first DC-8-50 would cost $6,083,731 for March 1962 delivery. Twenty-one new orders brought the total to 172 at the end of 1961, with 154 already delivered.

A reduction in manufacturing led to substantial layoffs at Long Beach, so community leaders lobbied the local Congressman to solicit DC-8 orders from the U.S. Air Force, but his response was that no order would be forthcoming. He did suggest that ways be studied to provide financing for customer airlines, but Douglas had already done so. For example, the cost for Panair do Brazil's two DC-8-30s with spares, training and associated equipment, totaled $20.2 million, of which Douglas loaned $2.4 million and the United States Export-Import Bank provided $13.8 million; Panair paid the balance at delivery. This kind of financial packaging is considered quite normal, though U.S.-based airlines rely on commercial banks rather than the Export-Import Bank.

Former KLM DC-8-32 PH-DCD (ln 75/msn 45379), served with Martinair for several years. (P. Huxford)

The Supersonic Flight

On August 21, 1961, during a test flight to confirm performance data on the new 4 percent leading edge, a production DC-8-43 (ln 130/msn 45623) flew faster than the speed of sound. It occurred during a shallow dive over the Askania tracking range at Edwards Air Force Base, California, and was the first time a commercial jet airliner ever exceeded Mach 1.0.

This feat was not repeated until a Russian Tu-144 exceeded Mach 1.0 on June 5, 1969, followed by the prototype Anglo-French Concorde on October 1, 1969.

The idea of a DC-8 supersonic flight came from Bill Magruder, co-pilot on Ship One's maiden flight. Before this was attempted, a great deal of analytical work was done to determine the best entry speeds, dive angles, recovery initiation points, and other information.

The 130th DC-8 to be built, destined to become CF-CPG of Canadian Pacific Air Lines (CPA), bore the Douglas test registration N9604Z at the time. It was determined that stabilizer trim would be required to assist recovery because of expected low elevator effectiveness. Additionally, just over 5,000 pounds of ballast would be carried in the rear cabin to provide an aft center of gravity for assistance in maneuverability during the pull-out. No other special measures were needed.

To verify on-board test instrumentation, the DC-8 was accompanied by a Lockheed F-104 Starfighter with a closely calibrated instrument panel for accuracy. In addition, the Askania range provided radar and theodolite tracking assistance.

A weather balloon, fitted with radiosonde transmitters, verified the geometric height and barometric pressures as an additional accuracy check of aircraft instrumentation. It also indicated that the ambient temperature was minus 96.3 degrees Fahrenheit. To record the event on film, the flight was also accompanied by a two-seat North American F-100 Super Sabre provided by the Air Force Flight Test Center.

The flight-test crew on board this historic flight included Magruder, Paul Patten, Joseph Tomich, plus Flight Test Engineer Richard Edwards. The aircraft, powered by Rolls-Royce Conway R.Co.12 Mark 512 engines, took off from Long Beach with a gross takeoff weight of 188,000 pounds. The track for the dive was from the southern tip of Rogers Dry Lake, towards the southern tip of Rosemond Dry Lake. As the dive commenced, the DC-8 weighed 170,600 pounds, of which 31,300 pounds was fuel. The pushover was initiated at 52,090 feet and recovery commenced at 42,000 feet. During the pushover, a negative G force of 0.5 was held for 15 seconds and the dive angle maintained at 15 degrees. The aircraft was trimmed so that a 50-pound push was required to maintain the dive angle. The highest speed reached was Mach 1.012 (660.6 mph) at 41,088 feet, with a maximum true airspeed of 662.5 mph achieved at 39,614 feet. Full recovery was completed by the 36,000-foot level at Mach 0.95. Maximum G-loading was 1.70 during pullout. No buffeting was experienced throughout the transonic period, though some was experienced while decelerating through Mach 0.94 at 35,000 feet, and a mild "buzz" was recorded on the rudder tab and ailerons during the recovery.

Throughout the speed run, the engines were operated at maximum takeoff thrust levels. The airplane's regular production instrumentation recorded the correct speeds, but the Mach meter did not exceed Mach 0.96 during the supersonic portion of the flight.

The 52,090-foot altitude attained was also a record for commercial jet airliners at the time. This historic flight remains the only supersonic flight achieved by an airliner other than Concorde and the Tu-144. To commemorate the event, a small plaque was affixed to a bulkhead in CF-CPG. Sadly, after nearly 19 years of service with CPA, this historic aircraft was sold for scrap on March 17, 1980, having accumulated some 70,567 hours during 24,268 flights.

Chapter V
Turbo-Fan Power

Ship One after being re-engined with JT3D-1s.

The DC-8 Series 50

Even before the DC-8's first flight, Pratt & Whitney had continued development of the JT3, converting it into a turbo-fan engine. This new model, designated JT3D-1, created a better mix of air and fuel, resulting in improved combustion, higher thrust ratings and much lower fuel burn rates. To attach it to the airplane, a new pylon and engine pod were designed by Douglas. Calculations showed that with this new power plant, the DC-8 would exceed its performance guarantees. The improved fan system also reduced noise considerably, allowing elimination of the daisy-petal exhausts. The reverse-thrust system was modified to re-direct exhaust gases forward through a series of cascades and slots located aft of the hot section, normally covered when the reverser clamshell doors were stowed.

The reduced fuel requirement meant that heavier payloads could be carried over greater distances and, as the JT3D-1 thrust levels increased to 17,000 pounds, maximum takeoff weight was pushed up to 276,000 pounds, identical to the DC-8-21.

Conversion of Ship One to the Series 50 (model 51) prototype included all the aerodynamic improvements created since the first flight, except the 4-percent chord increase. Externally, it differed from earlier models only in the design of the engine pod and nacelle. In its new form, Ship One performed its maiden flight on December 20, 1960, piloted by Heimerdinger and Magruder.

From the beginning, Douglas offered two other versions of the Series 50, the 52 and 53, both powered by the JT3D-3B engine rated at 18,000 pounds static thrust, plus strengthened landing gear and the 4 percent leading edge. The model -52's MTOW was initially 300,000 pounds, later increased to 305,000 pounds, and 315,000 pounds on the -53.

Production of the DC-8-50 had been phased in prior to Ship One's first flight, so the initial production aircraft, a model 53 destined for KLM, was ready for delivery on April 3, 1961. Orders for the DC-8-50 were in hand from KLM,

Installation of JT3D-1 turbo-fan engines began with the Series 50 DC-8. Clean configuration is shown on the left. In the reverse-thrust mode (right), jet exhaust is redirected forward and outward while the rear section is sealed off.

DC-8-53 N9608Z (ln 155/msn 45608), **Pacific Pacer.**

Iberia, United Air Lines, National Airlines, Philippine Airlines, Trans Caribbean and Aeronaves de Mexico; most were the result of converting existing orders for Series 30 variants.

On April 21, the second production DC-8-53 for KLM flew nonstop from Long Beach to Rome in 11 hours, 17 minutes, establishing a new distance record of 6,890 miles. The flight continued on to Amsterdam, Caracas, and back to Long Beach as part of an FAA functional and reliability test. A type certificate was issued on April 28 for all three sub-variants and subsequently amended on October 10, 1961, to include versions modified with the 4-percent-leading-edge addition.

The introduction of a quieter engine was welcomed by airlines and airport managers alike. In January 1960, the Port of New York Authority instituted the first lawsuit against an airline – Delta – for continued failure to observe local noise regulations. The case was withdrawn shortly after Delta

began complying with the rules. In July 1960, the FAA announced a set of "voluntary" rules, agreed to by the airlines, to standardize noise abatement procedures which would apply to all turbojet and turboprop aircraft. The FAA also mandated the installation and use of flight data recorders by November 1, 1960.

DC-8 deliveries continued to decline in 1962, when only 22 were handed over to eight customers. Of these, only Philippine Airlines (PAL) and Aeronaves de Mexico were new DC-8 operators. The pair of model 53s for PAL were actually ready for delivery in November 1961, but a financing package was not in place at the scheduled delivery time. One airplane was stored, unpainted, until February 1962 when PAL finally closed the deal and leased the aircraft to KLM. The second DC-8 order was canceled and the aircraft stored. KLM purchased it in April 1962 for lease to PAL where the DC-8 spent most of its working life.

Trans Caribbean Airways DC-8-51 N8780R (ln 151/msn 45628), named **James Roy.**
After flying with several other carriers, it was broken up in May 1986 at Brussels.

After just three months with Interswede in 1971, Eastern Air Lines repossessed DC-8-51 SE-DCT (ln 151/msn 45628).
(Author's Collection)

In the interim, Douglas used the second ex-PAL aircraft to demonstrate the DC-8-50's payload/range capabilities. Ship 155, registered N9608Z, was painted in a special livery and named *Pacific Pacer*. On February 20, 1962, it completed a 4,840-mile nonstop flight from Seattle to Tokyo carrying a 41,005-pound payload. A navigator borrowed from Northwest, Robert Trap, assisted the Douglas crew of Heimerdinger, Patten and Tomich. Four cabin attendants and 51 passengers were also aboard, with the remainder of the payload being ballast. The return flight on February 23 set a new long distance record by flying nonstop from Tokyo to Miami — 8,792 miles — in 13 hours, 52 minutes. The takeoff weight was 297,500 pounds, including 155,000 pounds of fuel. Almost 10,000 pounds remained at engine shut-down. A top ground speed of 790 mph was reached about two hours after leaving Tokyo, thanks to jetstream winds. This easily beat the old distance record of 7,023 miles from Seattle to Beirut established earlier in the same month, suggesting that perhaps a bit of "one-upmanship" was in the air.

Also in February 1962, Douglas attained another important technical achievement when a DC-8 demonstrated its automatic landing capability to airline customers and U.S. Air Force representatives. Developed jointly by Douglas and Sperry Phoenix Co., it was a minor modification to the Sperry SP-30 automatic flight control system already fitted to all DC-8s. The new system allowed a "hands-off" operation from takeoff to touchdown and also permitted lower weather minima to be considered. Previous systems had operated only until the middle marker navigational beacon had been reached.

N916R (ln 223/msn 45753) served on Icelandair's routes to Scandinavia and the United Kingdom during the 1980s. Currently it flies with MK Airlines as 5N-MKE.
(Author's Collection)

Originally N8064U with United, DC-8-52 OB-R1287 (ln 228/msn 45759), Faucett's **Santa Isabelle** *was retired in January 1992 after nearly 54,000 flying hours.*

Travel club Points of Call Canada operated the former ZK-NZE (ln 336/msn 45985) of Air New Zealand during 1988-89. It now flies in a freighter configuration for LAC of Colombia, as HK-3842X.

Flown by Maldives Airways for only a year, 8Q-CAOO5 (ln 212/msn 45689) is seen in November 1984 prior to departure from Marana, Arizona, where it had been stored.

Evergreen International leased DC-8-52 N800EV (ln 128/msn 45301) to several airlines, including Northeastern.

(All photos this page Author's Collection)

47

Ship One:

The Original DC-8

Ship One, of no further use to Douglas for flight testing, was re-furbished and received a full passenger interior. Leased to National Airlines for a year commencing June 21, 1961, it was then sold to Trans International Airways (TIA). TIA operated the aircraft for several years and leased it to Lufthansa for North American charters during the summer of 1965. It then spent one year leased to CPA as CF-CPN before being sold to Delta, which restored the original N8008D registration. Purchased by F.B. Ayer in March 1979, it was leased to Aeromexico as XA-DOE until January 1982, then placed in storage at Marana, Arizona, where it remains at the time of writing. Ship One has accumulated a total of 60,918 hours in 32,411 flights to date. Five of the airlines that operated Ship One are shown on these pages.

(▲ Clay Jansson)

(▼ Author)

(▲ *Author*)

(▲ *Ray Leader*)   (▼ *Author's Collection*)

Later to become CF-TJL with Trans-Canada, the first DC-8-54JT (ln 175/45640) demonstrates its loading methods during a visit to Miami.

The Jet Trader

Carrying 176 passengers in a high-density configuration, plus a full cargo load in its belly, the DC-8's payload was approximately 40,000 pounds. With the Series 50 capable of lifting more than double this amount, Douglas decided to offer a freighter and also a combination passenger-freighter version, known as a "combi."

Donald Douglas, Sr. had surprised his audience at the Ship One rollout ceremonies when he announced his belief that the future of air cargo development lay in the use of jet freighters. He had quietly authorized the exploration of extending the DC-8's potential by installing a swing-tail plus

JET TRADER INITIAL SPECIFICATION		
Maximum take-off weight	(lb)	310,000
Maximum landing weight	(lb)	217,000
Maximum zero fuel weight	(lb)	128,500
Manufacturer's empty weight	(lb)	123,000
Operating empty weight	(lb)	128,500
Space limited payload	(lb)	62,610
Passengers (165lb each)		54
Flight crew		3
Cabin attendants		2
Fuel capacity	(USG)	23,397
Fuel capacity	(lb)	156,760

a large cargo door just aft of the cockpit to expedite ground handling. A strengthened floor structure and the addition of rollers, tie-downs, and other equipment were also to be incorporated. For a short while, this version was called the DC-8A, a name used earlier in the DC-8 program.

This concept came in part from an attempt by Douglas to elicit new military interest in a DC-8 variant which would fill a variety of roles. The airplane had already been demonstrated at several U.S. Air Force bases to high-ranking officers. Tentatively named "Jetmaster," the Douglas Model 1920 would be capable of operating as a freighter, troop carrier or medical evacuation aircraft with capacity for 67 litter patients plus 85 ambulatory passengers. Unfortunately for Douglas, approval had already been given to Lockheed-Georgia for the prototype C-141 Starlifter, which made its first flight in December 1963.

Douglas announced in October 1960 that the DC-8A would be offered with either JT3D or Rolls-Royce Conway engines, and would be launched provided that a minimum order for between five and 10 airplanes was received. A 1962 first flight was proposed.

In May 1961, Donald Douglas, Jr. gave the go-ahead to build a prototype DC-8-50CF, though it was marketed as the "DC-8F Jet Trader," with the first flight scheduled for August 1962 and delivery available the following December. Initially, the aircraft was designed to be a combi-freighter, with a fixed bulkhead to separate the passengers from the cargo. Approximately two-thirds of the fuselage would be for cargo, with the balance accommodating 54 tourist-class passengers. To minimize cost and save weight, the swing-tail concept was abandoned; cargo would be loaded through an

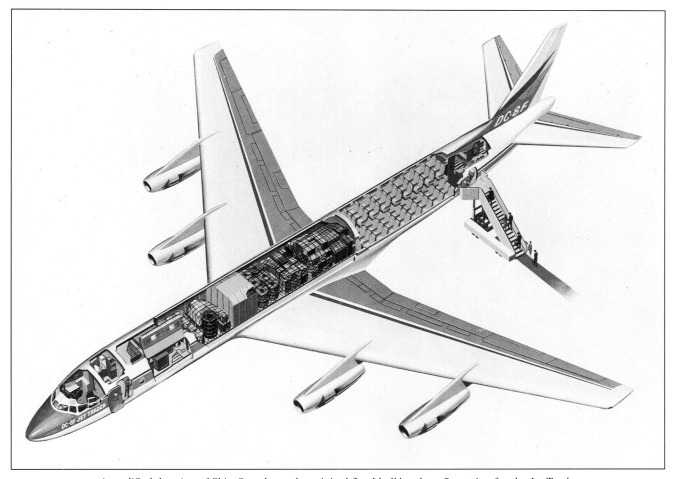

A modified drawing of Ship One shows the original fixed bulkhead configuration for the Jet Trader.

upward-opening, 86-inch by 140-inch door located just aft of the forward entry. The DC-8-50CF was intended to fly 3,100 miles with full reserves and carry 16 tons of freight, plus 54 passengers.

By September 1961, the design had evolved further, with the aft pressure bulkhead relocated an additional 76 inches aft, increasing its all-passenger capacity to 189; external dimensions were unchanged. To gain the additional space, the rear pressure bulkhead was changed from a dome shape to a flat panel. The cargo-passenger divider was now moveable, allowing 10 different configurations to be utilized, ranging from all-passenger to all-freight. Two new emergency exits were located aft of the wing to compensate for the inaccessible regular exits when the cargo bulkhead blocked access. New seats were designed for quick removal for stowage in the belly, while the hat racks were made to fold down against the sidewall. Forward toilets were located on pallets for easy removal, but the rear galley and toilets, aft of the rear door, were permanently installed. A reinforced floor and pallet-handling system allowed rapid handling of cargo. Installation of a cargo barrier net at the forward end of the freight compartment protected the crew against surge forces up to 9 Gs. The slightly heavier structure and beefed-up landing gear allowed an increase in the MTOW to 315,000 pounds, and the MLW from 176,000 pounds to 224,000 pounds. A combination of new brakes and anti-skid units, plus a revised ground spoiler system, reduced landing distances by more than 1,000

feet. The engine ultimately selected was the JT3D-3B turbofan, with 18,000 pounds of static thrust.

All-freighter and standard passenger-only variants were offered in addition to the convertible version. The fully convertible type could carry a 91,000-pound payload, while the passenger model lifted 50,000 pounds. However, the all-freighter, with passenger-related amenities omitted (including windows, air conditioning ducts, etc.), had a maximum payload of 96,000 pounds. The only buyer of the all-freighter DC-8-54AF was United, which eventually bought a total of 15. The "AF" is an unofficial designation; Douglas still referred to the stripped aircraft as the DC-8-54JT. Initially, all in-house documentation referred to the DC-8-54CF and the later DC-8-55CF, as the DC-8-54JT or DC-8-55JT, respectively. This designation applied to both convertible and all-freighter versions. The model 55s differed from the -54s only by an increased MTOW, to 325,000 pounds, made possible through further strengthening of the landing gear. The DC-8-55 was also sold in an all-passenger configuration, but as two lesser-known variants. JAL, Garuda and KLM all ordered Series 55 passenger aircraft, but wanted the fuselage interior to be the same as the Series 30s. This model did not have the rear bulkheads moved aft and were identified as -55L. (The L stood for less aft bulkhead.) Conversely, SAS and VIASA elected to have -55s with the interior extension, so their aircraft were called DC-8-55ABs. (The AB stood for aft bulkhead).

An 88-inch-by-88-inch pallet is guided onto the roller mat inside a Jet Trader. Note the cargo restraining net to protect the crew.

The first Jet Trader order came on September 17, when state-owned Trans-Canada Air Lines indicated that it would order four DC-8-54CFs and take options for two more. At the time, Canadair CL-44 turbo-prop production was slowing down, and a strong lobby was put forth by Canadair, demanding that the Canadian Government force TCA to buy CL-44 freighters instead. This action delayed confirmation of the Douglas order until December 1961. Interestingly, privately owned Canadian Pacific offered to take some CL-44s on condition that it be awarded new routes for their use, but the Government turned down the proposal.

Introduction of the convertible aircraft led to a new type of customer, the supplemental carrier. The first to place an order was Trans International Airlines (TIA), a military charter specialist, which signed up for two Series 50s plus an option for a third, on June 11, 1962. The first aircraft was for a model 52 to be accepted almost immediately, while the second would be a Jet Trader for delivery in April 1963. Trans Caribbean, already operating -53s, purchased two Jet Traders for 1963 delivery and KLM added three, raising its total to 13, plus an another model 53 option. In September, Delta, JAL and Iberia each added a Series 50, while Alitalia and CPA each picked up a Series 40, Swissair also announced a Series 50 order in October.

Meanwhile, the DC-8 continued to set speed records; a CPA example flew from Montreal to Rome in just 6 hours, 48

minutes during September 1962. By the year's end, orders had passed the 200 mark. A late surge of buying in December added 13 aircraft to the back-log, leading Douglas to increase the production and re-hire 1,200 employees. Repeat orders came from Air Afrique (two -53s), Alitalia (two -43s), Delta (two -51s), and Iberia (one -53). New customers included Capitol Airways, which bought two -54JTs, and Flying Tigers, which also selected two -54JTs; one was a previously unannounced Slick Airways order, later canceled. It was further announced that the total DC-8 flight hours passed the one million mark on October 13, 1962. TCA started 1963 by firming up an option for its fifth DC-8-54JT during the first week in January.

The first major used DC-8 transaction began in October 1962 when Northwest Airlines, standardizing its fleet with Boeing jets, sold one of its DC-8s to UAT, with the remaining four going to National Airlines in early 1963.

The first DC-8-54CF was Line Number 175, which made its maiden flight as N9609Z (later CF-TJL), on October 29, 1962, piloted by Magruder and George Jansen. FAA testing commenced on December 27, culminating in the type certificate being issued on January 29, 1963.

During the flight trials, it was confirmed that a 189-seat aircraft could be converted to an all-freighter configuration, fully loaded with pallets and dispatched in two hours. A 63-seat layout could be converted into a 123-seat configuration,

This version of the DC-8-55JT offered to the U.S. Air Force featured both forward and aft main deck cargo doors.

all cargo loaded and passengers boarded in 1 hour, 35 minutes.

In November 1962, at the request of the military, yet another attempt was made to sell DC-8s to the U.S. Air Force, this time with Jet Trader demonstrations at three military bases. It met with some interest. Defense Secretary Robert MacNamara requested a proposal for a "Multi-Mission DC-8F" in February 1963, and a bid was submitted for up to 200 aircraft. One of the missions envisioned was for AWACS (Airborne Warning and Control System). The aircraft, identified as Model D-887, carrying a 29-foot-diameter "roto-dome," would have been capable of staying on station for 9 hours within 500 miles of its base. A second version would have had a 35-foot-diameter roto-dome and could have loitered for 5.2 hours, 1,200 miles from base. MTOW would have been 323,000 pounds, with an operating empty weight of 150,000 pounds. Various other roles were proposed, including anti-submarine patrols, electronic counter measures, aerial refueling, medical evacuation, and cargo transport.

However, the decision was made to stay with Boeing's C-135, which was already well-established in the inventory.

In parallel with the 1963 proposal, the U.S. Air Force was also began looking for a twin-jet medical evacuation aircraft, a role which eventually fell to the C-9A Nightingale, a military version of the Douglas DC-9-30CF.

TCA took the first three of its Jet Traders within a three-week period beginning January 30, 1963; two were delivered with full complements of passenger seats. The flight-test aircraft was not handed over until April 24 when refurbishing and final interior installations were completed. TCA inaugurated the first-ever revenue jet service with a mixed passenger-cargo jet when its DC-8 Combi began flying the Montreal-Prestwick-London route on March 2, 1963. Initial services were flown with 117 economy seats and four 88-inch-by-108-inch freight pallets on the main deck.

TIA was the second airline to introduce the Jet Trader, taking delivery of its first aircraft in April. Trans Caribbean's two convertibles were also delivered during 1963, and normally operated in a combi role. Capitol Airlines, another U.S. supplemental, received a Jet Trader in September.

Douglas Finance Corporation (DFC) was established in February 1963 as a separate entity to help customers finance the purchase of new aircraft. Most were small, supplemental

TIA's first DC-8-54JT (ln 182/msn 45669), shortly after delivery at Oakland, California. (Clay Jansson)

Jet Trader N4904C (ln 187/msn 45668) of Capitol International arriving at London-Heathrow in September 1966. The aircraft remains in service today with Transportes Aereos Boliviana. (Author)

operators that relied on military contracts. Riddle Airlines, a financially strapped carrier, was the first to utilize this avenue, in August, signing a five-year lease for two Jet Traders plus spares, and an option to purchase, for $7.2 million each. Credit would be given for previously made lease payments if Riddle were to buy the airplanes later. One Jet Trader was delivered on September 20, making Riddle the first all-cargo airline to provide pure jet service. It operated in Riddle's colors for only a few months. After a stormy stockholder meeting in November, the airline reorganized and changed its name to Airlift International.

A secondary function of DFC was to assist foreign airlines with Export-Import Bank loan negotiations. The company still exists today as McDonnell Douglas Finance Corp. and has since expanded into many other types of business endeavors.

Meanwhile, several airlines began re-engining older model DC-8s, adding aerodynamic improvements as needed.

Delta, PAL and Swissair made the changes required to bring their fleets to the Series 50 standard and United upgraded nine model 11s to the -21 specification.

A notable event took place on May 22, 1963, when a TIA Jet Trader, operating a military cargo charter flight, flew from Travis AFB, California to Saigon with a record 87,000 pounds of cargo. Several fuel stops were made en route. Swissair, after accepting its first model 53 in October, also set a new record by flying from Long Beach to Beirut, a distance of 7,460 miles, in less than 14 hours.

On July 20, Douglas became involved in an unusual joint venture with the National Geographical Society, U.S. Navy, and several other corporations. A DC-8-51, contributed by Delta, cruised at 42,000 feet over northern Canada while following the shadow of a solar eclipse, prolonging for those aboard the period of total darkness across the sun. Several windows were modified to accept various types of instrumentation and camera equipment. In addition, minuscule

Although Riddle was re-named Airlift International in 1964, its first Jet Trader, N108RD (ln 189/msn 45663), retained its old titles through at least March 1965. (Clay Jansson)

DC-8-51 N801E (ln 14/msn 45408) was converted from a model 12 shortly before its mission on behalf of the National Geographic Society.

meteorite samples were collected via a special fitting designed to collect air samples. A number of well-known scientists from several countries were invited to observe the eclipse. The aircraft, N801E, had just been re-engined, bringing it from a model 21 to a -51. It re-entered service with Delta on September 18, 1963.

In May 1963, United committed to three Series 50AFs for 1964 delivery and KLM signed up for two -50CFs in June. Tasman Empire Air Lines (TEAL) ordered three DC-8-53s and Delta added two -51s in August, followed by two more in November. Japan Air Lines also added two more -53s and bought its first -55CF.

Part of the incentive to continually improve the DC-8 was ongoing competition from Boeing. For example, in mid-1963 Boeing tried to persuade SAS to trade its DC-8-33s for an all-Boeing fleet of 707-320B/C and B727-100 equipment, which would also replace the Caravelles. SAS was happy with the French twin-jets, so declined on the 727, and elected to stay with the DC-8 by ordering two -55s in November 1963. This kind of high-stakes competition was and continues to be routinely undertaken.

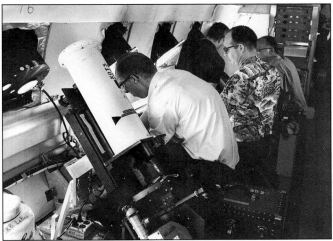

The DC-8 was extensively modified to accommodate scientists aboard this special flight.

By the end of 1963, total deliveries had reached 192, with 24 unfulfilled orders on the books. Of the 19 DC-8s delivered that year, 10 were Jet Traders, three were Series 40s for Alitalia and CPA, the balance Series 50s. Air Afrique, the only new customer, received its first Series 50, having previously wet-leased DC-8-30s from TAI.

Douglas now felt more comfortable about the long-term prospects of the DC-8 program. The rate of new orders had fluctuated considerably over the past several years, but began to stabilize at a rate which would generate at least $100 million in sales per year. The company had already spent $260 million in development costs, so the break-even point was still in the future. Of the 216 airplanes sold, 107 were ordered in 1955 and 1956, followed by a total of only 62 over the next five years. 1962, as mentioned, was a good year with 26 sales and 1963 ended almost as strong, with 21. The 1962 and 1963 totals were boosted by 17 Jet Trader purchases.

After its initial assignment as a test bed for the new JT3D engine pods, DC-8-54JT (ln 201/msn 45674) was delivered to Airlift International.

United was the only carrier to receive standard body pure freighter DC-8s from the factory. N8045U, a model 54JT (ln 235/msn 45801), at Chicago-O'Hare in August 1980.
(Author)

Formerly with Braniff, this DC-8-54JT (3D-ADV, ln 274/msn 45858) served many carriers prior to joining African International.
(Author's Collection)

Above: Trans Caribbean flew its DC-8s in three different liveries. DC-8-54JT N8783R (ln 195/msn 45684) displays the final example in the above photo. (Paul Huxford)
Below: The same aircraft later migrated to the UK where it joined IAS Cargo Airlines, becoming G-BDDE. Because of high certifications costs in that country, only two British carriers operated DC-8s. (Author's Collection)

TAAG Angola leased this DC-8-55JT 9Q-CKI (ln 208/45683) from Lukim Air Services in 1986. (Author's Collection)

Latin America has become a haven for many used DC-8s. This model 51F (HK-3816X, ln 204/msn 45685) appears in the colors of ATC. (via Eddy Gual)

Originally for Eastern Air Lines, DC-8-51 N875C (ln 163/msn 45635) was delivered to National on April 6, 1962. (Clay Jansson)

Fluctuating Fortunes

In 1960, Douglas entered into an agreement to market and provide product support for the French-built Sud Caravelle, which was the first short-medium range jet to be offered to the airlines. Sud had already sold 20 examples to United, and Douglas negotiated a letter of intent with TWA in February 1961. However, Boeing launched its 727 program in late 1960, and TWA subsequently canceled the Caravelle order in June 1962, ordering a fleet of 727s instead. Eastern and United had already ordered 40 each. Shortly afterwards, the Douglas-Sud agreement was terminated.

Another interesting occurrence took place in January 1963, which was to have a major impact on the future of Douglas. Anxious to enter the commercial aircraft market,

James S. McDonnell, Chairman of McDonnell Aircraft Company, quietly acquired 300,000 shares of Douglas' common stock. He approached Douglas Jr. and Sr. with a merger proposal, at a meeting in Palm Springs, California. The proposal offered one share of McDonnell stock for two shares of Douglas common stock, but the plan was soundly rejected.

By coincidence, Douglas had been looking at the twin-jet airliner market for some time and had recently decided to press ahead with its own product, designated Model 2086, which the advanced design group had been working on for some time. Senior management felt able to take this step because the 1962 fiscal year had yielded over $10 million in profit, the first in several years. It was thought that costs would be minimized by involving several risk-sharing subcontractors. So, during the meeting with Mr. McDonnell, he was offered the opportunity to build the wing. He declined,

N801SW (ln 207/msn 45692) was one of four model 54JTs operated by Seaboard World prior to delivery of DC-8-63CFs. It later served with the French Air Force and is currently employed by MK Airlines as 9G-MKC.

Cyprus Airways leased DC-8-52 N99862 (ln 141/msn 45303) from McDonnell Douglas. Originally with United, the aircraft had been trad-ed-in against DC-10 equipment in 1971 by Air New Zealand. (Author's Collection)

Saturn leased DC-8-54JT N3325T (ln 225/msn 45754) from Trans-International in 1969 for one year. It crashed in Quito, Ecuador, on September 18, 1984, while in service with AECA as HK-BKN. (Jeff Burch)

and an agreement was later reached with de Havilland Canada, which would not only build the wings, but also the rear un-pressurized section of the fuselage and vertical stabilizer. Similar agreements were rapidly reached with sub-contractors both at home and abroad. In February 1963, Douglas announced the launch of the DC-9 program. Early success came through selling 15 to Delta Air Lines in May, but otherwise sales were very slow, with only 57 sold prior to the first flight in February 1965.

Douglas engineers elected to manufacture both the DC-8 and DC-9 on a single integrated production line. DC-8s appeared to have a steady market of between 20 and 25 per year, and company management believed that the DC-9 market would yield about 500 over a 10-year period. This vastly

underestimated forecast was to cause great problems in the following three years.

DC-8 sales unexpectedly slumped again, when only 14 new orders were booked during 1964. Just three Jet Traders were sold (two to Trans Caribbean and one to Trans International), plus two model 51s to Delta. United saved the day by picking up six model 52s and three Series 50AFs. Deliveries for the year totaled just 20, including the first Series 50AF to United. Initial deliveries of Jet Traders were made to Seaboard World and KLM. Once again, the company was forced to gamble by developing new models of the DC-8 to keep the line open.

A major DC-8 customer, Spanish carrier Iberia accepted EC-BAV (ln 258/msn 45814) on April 21, 1966.

Inset: *Following its duties as Pacific Pacer (see Page 45), this DC-8-53 (ln 155/msn 45608) was leased by KLM to Philippine Airlines. PAL and KLM often operated joint services.*
(Author's Collection)

F-BJLB (ln 83/msn 45568) was delivered to UAT on August 5, 1960, as a model 33, and upgraded to -53 standards two years later. UAT joined TAI in 1963, to become UTA.

Chapter VI
Stretching The Eight

The Series 60 Evolves

As early as 1962, Douglas had begun looking at ways to stretch the aircraft and increase range. Most of the effort centered on taking advantage of the high gross-weight capabilities of the DC-8-55. Traffic growth showed that even larger aircraft were needed, especially in three major U.S. markets: transcontinental, West Coast-Hawaii and New York-Puerto Rico.

The simple solution was to trade fuel for payload by stretching the fuselage while retaining the existing wings, engines, landing gear, empennage and operating weights. Douglas was able to do this because of the DC-8's relatively high ground clearance of 63 inches, which reduced the danger of a tail strike on rotation. Also, the modest 30-degree sweepback and enlarged leading-edge slots contributed to a low angle of attack on takeoff. A 200-inch plug was inserted forward of the wing and a 240-inch plug added aft, resulting in an overall length of 187 feet, 4 inches. Major structural changes were needed to accommodate the bending forces created by added length. Fuselage skin gauges were increased fore and aft of the wing, and lower fuselage longerons had to be strengthened. To offset the additional structure weight, an intensive weight-saving program shaved 2,000 pounds from the earlier design by numerous small modifications, such as replacing metal wiring conduits with plastic where possible.

Passenger capacity was increased to 251 in an all-coach, six-abreast arrangement, with a 34-inch seat pitch. Cabin changes included relocating passenger conveniences to overhead,

substituting pull-down window shades for curtains and adding standard airline-type seats mounted on dual floor tracks. Initially, Hardman seats were selected, but any seat manufacturer's chairs could be installed at the customer's request. Two additional three-quarter size (type one) doors were located aft of the trailing edge to meet emergency evacuation requirements. The FAA eventually approved the carriage of up to 269 passengers, a number dictated by the number of people who could evacuate the aircraft in less than 90 seconds using half the available exits. This requirement was demonstrated in trials in a darkened hangar.

Design experience from the newer DC-9 program was incorporated in the cockpit. A DC-9-type instrument panel became standard, and the pilot-designed DC-9 control wheel was added. Solid state instrumentation was installed for the first time, and cockpit lighting changed from the red, used in earlier DC-8s, to white, as with the DC-9. Baggage racks were also identical to the twin-jet.

The only aerodynamic change made was a slight alteration to the relative position of the flaps and vanes to the wing, which created a minor reduction in flap-down drag without affecting lift. Other changes included boosting the capacity of the four generators from 20- to 30-kilovolt amperage and increasing the air-conditioning output to handle increased cabin volume. The belly pit cargo doors were enlarged to 56 inches by 60 inches from the standard DC-8's 36-inch-by-44-inch opening, and designed to slide up. In addition to passenger baggage, the cargo compartment could hold 15,000 pounds of freight. Designated as the DC-8-61 this new model retained the Series

CP Air's DC-8-63 CF-CPQ (ln 334/msn 45928) has migrated to Airborne Express, and remains one of the few unconverted -60s. (Author's Collection)

50's JT3D-3B engines and was to be certificated at the DC-8-55 performance levels, even though flight tests proved that its performance was better.

The DC-8-62

Despite all the aerodynamic improvements to the Series 50 wing, the company was still not satisfied that drag had been reduced to the absolute minimum. Ongoing research and wind-tunnel testing of models indicated that re-design of the engine pods and pylons would make a significant improvement in drag reduction.

Radical changes to the pod were proposed. Relocating the heat exchangers from the pod to the pylon reduced the pod's maximum diameter by 12 percent and its length by 8 inches. Two full-length ducts were added to carry fan air from the JT3B-3B fan-side ports along the entire length of the nacelle to a concentric exit nozzle around the primary exhaust nozzle, hence the name "long duct fan."

A 55-inch-long bullet placed in the primary exhaust nozzle to smoothly blend the primary and secondary exhaust streams also helped reduce noise levels. On the earlier DC-8-50 pod, the ducts exhausted the fan air on each side, three feet aft of the fan. The duct extension cut the drag losses caused by fan air exiting from the side nozzles, which had created shock waves, high negative pressures and scrubbing along the nacelle sides.

Considerable weight saving was achieved because the thrust-reverser requirement changed from three units (one each for the primary and side ducts) to one aft-mounted reverser with two rotating buckets. The wind-tunnel test results indicated a 5 percent improvement, but this was still considered insufficient.

Other tests demonstrated that the over-wing portion of the existing pylon produced negative high-pressure areas along the upper surface of the wing. By eliminating this part of the pylon and attaching it only to the underside of the wing, the problem was resolved.

To further lessen drag caused by the channeling effect of air passing between the two installations, the new pylons were extended to bring the exhaust cone 40 inches farther forward, almost directly under the wing leading edge. These changes reduced overall drag by another 5 percent.

Armed with these results, Douglas engineers reasoned that the MTOW could be raised yet again, this time to 335,000 pounds, allowing a major increase in performance. Douglas had been under pressure from European DC-8 operators, particularly SAS, to produce an aircraft capable of flying nonstop to the U.S. West Coast. Two Douglas executives, Jackson R. McGowen and Harry Hjorth, developed the basic design in a Stockholm, Sweden hotel room. To meet the challenge, a 3-foot extension to each wing tip was added, allowing storage of more fuel which, with revised leading-edge tanks, increased capacity by almost 900 gallons. The tip extension reduced drag by increasing the aspect ratio (the relationship of the span to the mean chord of a wing) from 7.0 to 7.52.

Maximum range, carrying a full load of passengers, was more than 6,000 miles. In addition to meeting range requirements, enough performance remained to permit an 80-inch stretch to the DC-8-50 fuselage, and 40-inch plugs were added fore and aft of the wing, allowing improved seating pitch, but the exit limits remained at 189 passengers. Other changes included slightly increasing the length of the leading edge slots and incorporating the same systems and cabin improvements proposed for the model 61. In addition, a new

N109RD (ln 201/msn 45674) showing the new long-pod nacelles mounted on existing pylons.

Eastern DC-8-63PF N8759 (ln 433/msn 46058), a variant unique in its initial lack of a main deck cargo door.

lighter, non-castoring main landing gear bogie was designed to take the increased weight. It would become known as the DC-8-62.

To confirm the new configuration, four hand-built pods were fitted to the existing pylons of a Jet Trader and flown in April 1964. The aircraft, N109RD, was destined for Airlift International, but for the test program it carried the titles "Douglas Ducted Fan DC-8." The flights confirmed the predicted performance improvement with no real surprises, and also demonstrated a significant reduction in noise compared to the un-ducted installation. Before being delivered to Airlift, N109RD was restored to the standard Series 50 engine pod installation.

The next step was to marry the bigger wing and long-duct pods with the stretched fuselage, which produced the DC-8-63 model. Though originally intended to have the same power plants as the model 62, the -63 was upgraded with JT3B-7 engines, rated at 19,000 pounds static thrust, allowing an MTOW increase to 350,000 pounds for the passenger model and 355,000 pounds for the freighters. It could carry

the maximum of 269 passengers over a 4,500-mile sector. Part of the reason for the shorter range of the model 63 was an increase in drag over the -62 created by the larger "wetted" area of the stretched fuselage. This drag penalty was calculated to be about 5 percent, but flight testing showed only a 2 percent penalty.

For increased comfort, most high-density aircraft normally operated in a 249-seat configuration. A typical mixed-class layout was 24 first-class seats at a 37-inch pitch and 186 in coach at a 34-inch pitch. Economics had lowered the airline industry's comfort level drastically since the first jets had entered service, but ticket prices had also declined with the advent of mass-market air travel.

The established Douglas practice of offering convertible and all-freighter versions was continued and substantially increased total sales. One unusual version was the DC-8-63PF. Manufactured as a passenger aircraft, the wing structure and landing gear were built to the stronger freighter standard. Eastern Air Lines was the only customer for this version, buying six. The philosophy was that the aircraft could

ONA's DC-8-55JT N852F (ln 269/msn 45856) Flagship Contender.

be easily and cheaply converted to a freighter without the penalty of carrying the added weight of a main-deck cargo door and its mechanism during normal passenger service. In addition, the purchase price was lower than the model 63CF. Four were subsequently converted to freighters. Of the remaining two, one was destroyed in flight by a bomb over Chad in 1984, and the other crashed after takeoff at Gander in 1985.

Boom Time Again

1965 was a year to remember at Long Beach. The DC-9 made its maiden flight on February 25, and orders poured in, reaching a total of 228 by year's end. DC-9 production and flight testing accelerated rapidly towards a goal of certification and service startup before December 31. The DC-9-10 received its type certificate on November 23, and entered service with Delta less than two weeks later. Meanwhile, the DC-8 also had its most successful year to date.

Douglas officially launched the "Super Sixty" series on April 4, 1965, with an initial order from SAS for four DC-8-62s plus four options, reserved as combi or freighter versions. The first sales of the -61 came just a few days later when United contracted for five, plus four model 52s and options for three Series 50AFs. Almost immediately thereafter, Eastern followed with an order for eight -61s. Jack McGowen, then deputy general manager of Douglas Aircraft Division, optimistically forecast a world-wide market for 500 Super Sixties, of which around 25 percent would probably be model 61s, with the remainder about evenly split between the model 62 and -63. A decision was made to increase the production rate to five a month by October 1966 as the Series 50 backlog had also improved in the past few months.

At year-end, Douglas salesmen had signed contracts for 38 Series 60s and 36 Series 50s, including 12 Jet Traders and three freighters. In spite of the considerable sales success, cash flow again became a problem and efforts were made to raise an additional $75 million in new capital and expand the

revolving credit line. The company had invested heavily in the new DC-9 program, pushed the DC-8 break-even point out again through developing the Series 60, and hired huge numbers of production workers. As the orders rolled in, it became apparent that the joint DC-8/DC-9 production line would have to be separated into a single line for the DC-8 and a twin track for the DC-9, requiring more unexpected capital.

Another unanticipated problem resulted from the DC-9's initial success. Eastern asked Douglas to build a stretched model, which required modifications – and more investment – to the wing, produced by de Havilland Canada (deHC). This new model, the DC-9-30, brought the aircraft into direct competition with the British-built de Havilland Trident. As a result, the British parent company was not eager to invest additional money in the DC-9 program. Douglas had little choice but to buy out the deHC share at a total cost of $86 million and reach agreement with the Canadian government to take over the Malton, Ontario facilities. Douglas Aircraft of Canada, Ltd. was formed on December 1, 1965, with approximately 4,000 ex-deHC employees.

In addition, Fleet Manufacturing, another Canadian subcontractor that built the ailerons and flaps, was beset with financial difficulties and had to be bailed out by Douglas.

During 1965, thirty DC-8s were delivered. TEAL, which later changed its name to Air New Zealand, took possession on July 19, and the last model 43s were delivered to CPA and Alitalia. Capitol, Flying Tigers, PAL and VIASA joined the ranks of DC-8 operators that year.

When Winston Churchill died in early 1965, *Life* magazine wanted to devote an entire special edition to his life and include photos of the state funeral in color. The publisher's normal deadline for color was Wednesday, but the funeral was on a Saturday. The problem was resolved by delaying the deadline to Saturday night, and having the funeral photos processed and edited in the air. A contract was worked out with Seaboard World to provide a DC-8 Jet Trader, which would be fitted out with a complete photo-processing and editing facilities. To ensure everything would fit into the

Air New Zealand's DC-8-52s carried the predecessor's TEAL identity for some time after the official name change.

Air Afrique's DC-8-53 TU-TCP (ln 83/msn 45568) started life as a -32 with UAT.
It was re-engined in 1965. See lower photo, Page 60. (Author's Collection)

Formerly with National as N779C, Braniff International DC-8-51 N814BN
(ln 174/msn 45644) was retired in 1982 and sold for scrap. (Harry Sievers)

Seen at New York-Idlewild, Alitalia DC-8-43 I-DIWM (ln 222/msn 45755), while
operating for VIASA, was sub-leased to KLM during the summer of 1963. (Author)

KLM's "Blue Top" color scheme came into use while DC-8s, such as this model
53 (PH-DCI, ln 123/msn 45613) were still in service. (Author's Collection)

Former United DC-8-52 N8064U (ln 228/msn 45759) flew briefly with Cayman Airways in 1974. (Author's Collection)

plane, the outline of the available cabin space was chalked out on a hangar floor at Chicago's O'Hare Field, and all the equipment was assembled there. When N8904C of Capitol Airways arrived, it was comparatively easy to quickly put everything in the correct location. As the aircraft arrived at Heathrow and was refueled, the film was brought aboard. Once airborne, processing began, fortunately lacking any of the vibration problems previously predicted. When the aircraft arrived at Chicago in the evening, all the page layouts were completed and ready to go to press.

In June 1965, the Port of New York Authority (PNYA) sent a letter to airlines using JFK, urging "the greatest care in ordering stretched versions of the DC-8 and 707." Trans-Caribbean was in the awkward position of having to sign a purchase agreement with Douglas by October 29 in order to lock in the price, delivery positions, and acceptable financing, as interest rates were about to increase. The airline wrote back, requesting PNYA's approval to operate several DC-8-61CFs that it was about to order. Trans-Caribbean, along with many other airlines, received a letter from the PNYA on October 28, stating that the DC-8-61 would probably be banned due to high noise levels being anticipated. However,

Shown just prior to the DC-8-61's first flight (left to right): Project Pilot Don Mullin, Chief Test Pilot Heimie Heimerdinger, Flight Test Engineer Dick Edwards, and Flight Engineer Joe Tomich.

Douglas assured the airline that the model 61 would be no worse than the -55JT, so Trans Caribbean placed its order at the agreed upon deadline. Eastern was also very perturbed, having just negotiated for five -61s. The airline's president, Floyd Hall, responded that no noise-level difference existed, since the model 61 was the same weight as the -55JT. In addition, Eastern -61s would operate under the MTOW, not needing a full fuel load for flights to Miami, its principal market. Also, seating would total only 198 in two classes, further reducing takeoff noise.

Continued Success — But

The first DC-8-61, registered N8070U, rolled out January 24, 1966, and made its maiden flight on March 14, in the hands of Don Mullin and Heimie Heimerdinger. Flight engineers Joe Tomich and Richard Edwards were also aboard the flight that lasted 4 hours, 45 minutes. The aircraft lifted off at 137 knots after a 4,600-foot ground roll. Takeoff weight was 255,000 pounds. After climbing to 31,000 feet, the aircraft flew to Palmdale Airport where a number of touch-and-go landings were accomplished before returning to Long Beach. Some windows were equipped with quick de-pressurization valves to ease crew escape in case of emergency. The pilots reported that handling was not much different from the standard DC-8.

In April, the PNYA again wrote to Douglas and the airlines to re-affirm its concern regarding takeoff noise of the DC-8-61, and indicated that it might still ban the aircraft from JFK. Eastern was now very concerned as it had already added more model 61s to its order and was about to raise the total again when the letter arrived. So it was finally agreed that the only solution would be to provide a demonstration of the aircraft at JFK. When the first Eastern aircraft was delivered March 3, 1967, noise measurements were taken for analysis and found to be slightly less than the DC-8-55JT as predicted by Douglas.

At the same time this issue was raised, the PNYA also stated that the DC-8-63, then intended to operate at 335,000 pounds MTOW, would exceed the bearing limits of 430 psi allowable stress on the runways and taxiways. Fortunately,

APSA of Peru leased DC-8-52 OB-R-931 (ln 142/msn 45619) from Iberia in 1969. Iberia's domestic subsidiary AVIACO also operated the aircraft for several years as EC-ARC. Later it passed through numerous owners, including The Lord's Airline, but never flew in its colors. *(Author's Collection)*

Although painted in TAE colors, ex-Delta DC-8-51 EC-DKH (ln 24/msn 45412) was never delivered to the carrier. *(Author's Collection)*

This former Air Canada DC-8-61 now flies with Kalitta /American International as -61F N813CK (ln 310/msn 45893).
(Author's Collection)

the warning came early enough for Douglas to revise the main landing gear "footprint" by having the tires 31.25 inches apart instead of the 30 inches on earlier models. Tire contact area increased from 200 square inches to 220 square inches to reduce the pressure.

The second model 61, in United colors, joined the test program in July and was used to qualify the autopilot. It was followed by a third in September which did some route proving flights. The first two had stripped interiors with test instrumentation installed, but the third was ready for airline use. In all, model 61s were to make 124 test flights totaling 175 hours flying before a type certificate was issued on September 1, 1966. Test pilots and United crews who flew the model 61 all reported that it demonstrated quicker takeoff, faster climb and shorter landing performance than the standard DC-8. The longer fuselage also made the aircraft more stable. On August 16, a -61 test flight flew from Long Beach to Tokyo in 11 hours, 50 minutes, then Tokyo to Winnipeg in 11 hours, on August 18.

By the end of the first quarter of 1966, the company was back in the black with the highest profits recorded since the DC-8's first flight. Military programs did well and contributed most of the profits. The corporate backlog stood at over $3 billion and outstanding debt was down to $24 million. Douglas even went so far as to close down its line of credit with the banks. On the negative side, the company lost out to Lockheed on the C-5A contract, and did not recognize that the 400-seat airliner market was coming until Pan Am ordered its first batch of Boeing 747s in April. A 650-seat double-decker aircraft, tentatively identified as the DC-10 was being studied, but the airline industry thought the project was too ambitious. Shortly thereafter, the advanced design group initiated the current DC-10 design in response to an American Airlines request which began as a twin-engine wide body with a 2,000 mile range, seating 250 in a mixed-class configuration.

In the second quarter of 1966, things changed for the worse. The escalating Vietnam War created a huge impact on the aircraft industry, and production of military aircraft became a major priority, to the detriment of the commercial manufacturers. Almost every item sub-contracted or vendor-provided was in short supply and more expensive. However, the biggest problem was power plant availability. For the next

two years, it was not unusual to see rows of DC-8s parked on the apron with concrete blocks hanging from the engine mounts while the aircraft were slowly completed. DC-9 production was similarly slowed. The "out of position" work, caused by jobs not completed at the scheduled line position, reached a crisis stage, and added considerably to costs. Inevitably, delivery delays got longer despite round-the-clock efforts to keep the aircraft moving. Hiring reached an all-time high, but skilled labor was in short supply, forcing the company to train workers with no experience. This was time-consuming and expensive. Compounding these problems was the proliferation of aircraft models offered by a sales-oriented management and the old Douglas tradition of configuring aircraft to individual customer requirements.

Less than 50 DC-9s were delivered in 1966, far short of the anticipated number; some were three months late. Earlier in the year, the company had written off the $100 million in DC-9 development costs, a standard accounting method of Douglas, Sr., who believed that such costs should be cleared from the books as soon as possible. Because of the problems described, each DC-9 delivered created a $500,000 loss. In addition, a number of key manufacturing and planning management officials left the company due to personality clashes, seriously affecting control of the situation.

The first DC-8-62 rolled out on June 28, by which time total DC-8 orders had reached 396; 101 orders and 37 options were for Series 60s. The new model took to the air for the first time on August 29, captained by Paul Patten and assisted by Don Mullin as co-pilot and Steve Benya as flight engineer. Two flight-test engineers were also aboard for the five-hour mission. The test-schedule was nearly identical to that of the model 61 and, by early October, 26 flights had been completed, totaling over 75 hours aloft. In December, Mullin, during a test flight at Yuma, Arizona, made the first takeoff at a gross weight of 350,000 pounds.

During a series of tests, the airspeed was gradually built up to 415 knots, with no sign of any problems, but at 418 knots, violent flutter in the wings suddenly erupted. The aircraft was immediately slowed down and returned to base for examination. The cause was traced to the new slimmer pylons, which were more flexible than the earlier version, and the cantilevered location of the engine pod. The problem was solved by re-design of the fuel management system, which

Air Transport International (ATI) now operates this former Air Canada model 61, as DC-8-61F N861PL (ln 364/msn 45964).
(via Eddy Gual)

Loftleidir operated many stretched DC-8s on its low-cost trans-Atlantic flights, including N8962T, a model 61CF (ln 316/msn 45900).
(Author's Collection)

Aeroflot-Armenian DC-8-61 (ln 315/msn 45912) wears the Nigerian registration 5N-HAS; photographed at Shannon in August 1991.
(Malcolm Nason)

Charter carrier Hispania leased Nationair DC-8-61 C-GMXB (ln 359/msn 45943) for two months in 1988. (Frank Duarte)

allowed retention of reserve fuel in the outer portion of the wing, thereby increasing its stiffness.

Flight testing also showed that the new engine installation had improved fuel efficiency by 8.5 percent over the DC-8-50, 2.5 percent better than predicted. This translated into a 2,000-pound increase in payload over the design range of 5,350 miles. Improved takeoff performance, which reduced field-length requirements by 2,000 feet, was created by slight repositioning of the double-slotted flap vanes relative to the wing. The long-duct pod reduced the takeoff noise by 2.5 decibels, and approach noise by 4.5 decibels below the Series 50 levels.

Meanwhile, the "standard" DC-8 was approved by the FAA for Category 2 auto-couple approaches and landings on October 17, lowering the pilot's decision point to an altitude of 100 feet with 1,200 feet of horizontal visibility. This was half the previously allowed minimum conditions.

Throughout all this mayhem, the sales force continued to have great success in 1966, with the DC-8 as well as the new DC-9, which reached a backlog of over 500 by year end. Ironically, this success compounded the difficulties. Contracts were being signed for delivery dates that were impossible to meet. (See Table).

By the end of the third quarter of 1966, losses had increased to $19 million for the year, and the lending banks were reluctant to advance any money, in spite of the huge backlog; the company faced bankruptcy. Many alternate sources of funding were explored but, in the end, outside financial advisors proposed the only viable solution: a merger. In spite of these woes, 69 DC-9s and 32 DC-8s were delivered in the

Order Book – December 1965

Model	55	50JT	50AF	61	61CF	62	62CF	63
Aeromexico	3							
Air Afrique	1							
Air Canada		2		4				
Alitalia						3		
Panagra*						4	1	
Capitol		1						
CPA	1							
Delta	4			3				
Eastern				5				
Garuda	1							
Japan Airlines	3							
KLM	2	1						2
MEA**						3		
National				1				
ONA		2						
SAS		1				4	1	
Seaboard		4						
Swissair						1		
Trans America						2		
Trans Caribbean						2		
UTA		1						
United	4		3	5				
VIASA	2							
Total	21	12	3	18	4	15	2	2

* The Panagra order was later transferred to Braniff when the two airlines merged on February 1, 1967.

** MEA order was canceled in late-1966.

DC-8-61CF N868F (ln 329/msn 45950) of ONA migrated to United Parcel Service. (H.J. Schroder)

Originally built for National Airlines, DC-8-61 F-GDPS (ln 352/msn 45981) was used by Point Mulhouse (also known as Point Air) for inclusive tour charters. (Eddy Gual)

Sub-leased from Minerve, DC-8-61 C-FCMV (ln 429/msn 46038) operated with Minerve-Canada from December 1987. (Eddy Gual)

Pacific East Air offered low-cost flights between California and Hawaii from 1982. When the carrier ceased operations in 1984, DC-8-61CF N867FT (ln 351/msn 45939) was returned to Flying Tigers. (Chuck Stewart)

Ex-Eastern DC-8-61 N8764 (ln 418/msn 46017) was operated by Capitol on its short-lived scheduled services in 1980-81. (Author)

One of several DC-8-61s acquired by JAL from Eastern Air Lines, N8768 (ln 350/msn 45983) is now owned by the GPA Group and leased to Emery. The aircraft has since been converted to a model 71F.   (S. Matsuzawa)

Birgenair operated DC-8-61 TC-MAB (ln 409/msn 46016) for five years. It now flies for Airborne Express as N843AX. (Author's Collection)

Saudia has leased many DC-8s for its cargo operations, including DC-8-61 N912R (ln 296/msn 45908). (Author's Collection)

All three of these Series 60 DC-8s eventually found their way to UPS after conversion to model 71F standards.
Top: *DC-8-61 N822E (ln 288/msn 45907) originally with Delta, now boasts over 70,000 flying hours.*
Center: *Universal Airlines DC-8-61CF N803U (ln 316/msn 45900) served with many carriers before its engine upgrade.*
Bottom: *Another -61CF, N8956U (ln 329/msn 45949) first flew with Saturn Airways.*

year, but at great cost. Sixteen examples were Jet Traders. Garuda was the only new customer, accepting a model 55 in July. Because of the delayed deliveries, United persuaded Douglas to paint one side of the first model 61 in the full United colors for its print publicity campaign. This was accomplished by covering the fuselage with colored paper to match the basic scheme, while preserving the house colors underneath.

DC-8-61 N8072U (ln 277/msn 45812) being dismantled in preparation for refurbishment. (Gerry Markgraf)

A New Name Emerges

Unfortunately, on December 31, 1966, just prior to being handed over to United, N8072U caught fire during final cabin cleaning. The third model 61 built, and first scheduled for delivery to United, it was quickly towed away from two others parked nearby, averting a catastrophe. Damage was limited to the fuselage area above the floor line. The airplane was re-built and accepted by United on February 17, 1968.

Because the first two aircraft were still full of test gear, the first DC-8-61 delivery to United did not occur until the fourth aircraft was handed over on January 26, 1967, following FAA approval for Category 2 approaches and landings on January 8. Also approved was a system to allow the auto-pilot to accomplish a fully automatic go-around if the landing could not be completed safely.

United inaugurated DC-8-61 service between Los Angeles and Honolulu on February 25; Eastern followed on March 3, between New York and San Juan. There were concerns initially that the much larger aircraft would create ground-handling problems, but additional ground staffing soon alleviated this. Difficulty operating the new baggage doors was at first thought to be attributable to the flexing of

United Air Lines developed a special cabin interior for its DC-8-61 Hawaii service. (UAL)

Trans International's DC-8-61CF N8961T (ln 294/msn 45902) on an early test flight.

the fuselage. However, modifications to the locking mechanism solved the problem. The advent of the model 61s led to the introduction of enhanced mechanized baggage handling in terminal buildings because of the increased baggage volume. Passenger boarding was handled by each customer in its own way, but most elected to use both front and rear doors, parking parallel to the terminal which usually took up two gate positions.

Meanwhile, several companies were approached with merger proposals. Among them, General Dynamics, North American Aviation, Martin Marietta and McDonnell Aircraft expressed interest. Later, Fairchild Aircraft and Signal Oil also made proposals. After all the competitive bids were considered by the Douglas Board of Directors, McDonnell was finally chosen, and an announcement was made on January 13, 1967. The Department of Justice approved the merger on April 26 and the new company, McDonnell Douglas, was officially in business on April 28.

While the negotiations were being held, Douglas maintained its delivery commitments. The first DC-8-63 was rolled out on March 6, wearing Douglas colors and registered N1503U. By then, 13 airlines had ordered a total of 42 model 63s. The first flight, lasting five hours, took place on April 10, in the hands of Cliff Stout and Harry Terrell. During the following two months, 73 flights totaling over 70 hours were completed.

On June 3, a model 63 took off from Edwards AFB at a gross weight of 361,150 pounds and landed at 355,400 pounds. During a test to determine the maximum brake energy at maximum

takeoff weights, the runway proved insufficient for the airplane to accelerate to 186 knots and then safely stop using maximum braking energy. A decision was made to take off, then land with 12 degrees of flaps and apply maximum braking as the aircraft slowed to the MTOW V2 speed. In service, MTOW was restricted to 355,000 pounds and maximum landing weight to 275,000 pounds, so this test confirmed that a considerable safety margin existed.

Order Book – December 1966

Model	50	50JT	61	61CF	62	62CF	63	63CF
Air Canada			2					
Air New Zealand	2							
Alitalia					7	2		
American Flyers					2			
Capitol	1							2
Canadian Pacific							4	
Delta			9					
Eastern			5					
Finnair						2		
Flying Tigers								10*
Iberia		1					2	1
Japan Airlines	1	1						
KLM							2	
National			2					
Philippine A/L	1							
Saturn					2			
SAS							2	
Seaboard								4
Swissair					2	1		
TIA			1					2
UTA					2			
United		6**	20					
Universal					2			
Total	5	8	38	7	11	5	10	19

* four -63CF and six -63AFs
** 50AF variants

National's first DC-8-61, N45090 (ln 296/msn 45908), appears in traditional red and blue livery during flight-test. The second example was delivered unpainted pending finalization of the carrier's new color scheme.

Certification of new models kept the flight-test department very busy during 1967. The DC-8-62 received its approval on April 27, and was followed by delivery of the first aircraft to SAS on May 3. It entered service between Copenhagen and New York on May 22. The prototype model 62, registered LN-MOO, also went to SAS on June 20, and later crashed into the sea while landing at LAX on the night of January 13, 1969.

By June 29, 1967, flight testing was completed and the model 63 type certificate issued by the FAA. Hand over of the first example, to KLM, came on July 15. A 10-hour, 30-minute ferry flight to Amsterdam was operated the following day; scheduled service on North Atlantic routes began July 27.

Japan Airlines started around-the-world DC-8 service on March 6, with twice-weekly flights in each direction.

The DC-8-61CF was certified on June 11, and entered service with Trans International Airlines on June 16. Braniff received its first DC-8-62CF on November 13, three days prior to the type's approval from the FAA.

The sales teams had not been idle either; 73 more Series 60s plus three -53s had been ordered.

With a new management team and influx of additional working capital, deliveries improved, and by the end of 1963,

41 DC-8s were handed over, no small achievement in the face of a continued shortage of parts. From the same final assembly building, 165 DC-9s were also delivered. However, these numbers were still lower than the revised schedule instituted by new management, calling for 55 DC-8s and 170 DC-9s.

DC-8 production included only two Series 50s, one -55 for JAL in September and a Jet Trader for Seaboard in October. In addition to SAS, Braniff and Alitalia also took delivery of their first DC-8-62s, on August 22 and October 28, respectively. Braniff's first aircraft was a DC-8-62CF, but it could only be operated as a passenger aircraft while awaiting formal model 62CF certification. It started -62 service on September 4, 1967, between New York and Buenos Aires. The remaining deliveries were versions of the model 61 which, in addition to United, went to Air Canada (Sept. 13), Trans Caribbean (December 6) and Saturn (December 28).

Shortly after Braniff put the DC-8-62 into service, a pilot over-rotated while taking off at La Paz, Peru. Without a tail skid its rear fuselage dragged along the ground. Finally airborne in the thin air – La Paz is one of the world's highest airports – the aircraft failed to pressurize, and was flown "down hill" to Lima, badly damaged. Douglas subsequently added a telescopic tail skid to all model 62s.

Finnair DC-8-62CF OH-LFR (ln 427/msn 46013) was re-registered OH-LFT only three months after delivery in 1969.

After a long career with United, DC-8-62 N8967U (ln 463/msn 46068 was converted to a -62F and currently serves with Canarias Air Cargo.

DC-8-62 JA8031 (ln 348/msn 45953) named Awaji, was delivered to JAL on April 19, 1968.

Swissair DC-8-62 HB-IDF (ln 319/msn 45920) is still flying with Buffalo Airways as a -62F, registered N923BV.

The second DC-8-61 for Japan Air Lines, JA8039 (ln 436/msn 46032) has its JT3B engines installed as Douglas works around the clock in January 1969.

Production Peaks

Flight test activity in 1968 was concentrated on freighter versions of the model 62 and 63, both of which were type-approved during the year. First to qualify was the DC-8-62CF on April 9. Alitalia received its initial convertible version the following day.

The DC-8-63CF first flew March 16 and, after 70 flights, was awarded type approval on June 10. Seaboard World took delivery of the test aircraft three weeks later and immediately put it into service on military contract work between the United States and the Far East. Seven days later, Flying Tigers received its first model 63CF. Performance of the type was considered ideal. It could carry a maximum freight load of 112,800 pounds over 2,700 miles. By now, the price tag had risen to around $12 million per aircraft.

Shortly after Flying Tigers put its -63s into service, the carrier reported that pilots were having braking problems when landing on wet runways at the 240,000-pound maximum landing weight. Douglas flooded a runway at its small Yuma, Arizona test center. During a series of high-weight landings, serious hydroplaning was experienced.

The problem was eliminated by improving the Hydrol Mark II anti-skid braking system, which was then re-designated Mark III and retrofitted to all DC-8-63s.

The last new version to leave the factory was the DC-8-63AF for Flying Tigers. The first of six was handed over on October 18, 1968. It could carry a 116,000-pound payload over 2,750 miles, this weight being limited only by the airplane's maximum landing weight. Flying Tigers, pleased with the efficiency of the model, said in a press release that the DC-8-63AF could pay for itself in just over a year. It assumed an $11 million aircraft making 16 round-trips per month, each flight grossing $53,000.

Sales of the DC-8 during 1968 fell off dramatically as the airlines began to anticipate the first 747 deliveries. In addition, the DC-10 program was launched February 28, followed by the Lockheed 1011 TriStar in April. Only thirty-two Series 60s were ordered during the entire year. (See Table.)

In contrast to low sales, production of the DC-8 reached a new peak during 1968 when deliveries totaled 101, versus a planned 91, putting the program back on schedule at last. DC-9 production was equally impressive with 206 handed over; three more than planned. These numbers were managed in spite of a comparatively small production line. A great deal of work was completed outside on the aprons surrounding the assembly hall before the aircraft were towed, at night, across Lakewood Boulevard to the flight ramp.

Among the deliveries were the last Series 50s. Air Canada received the final passenger version, a -53 on October 16, followed by a United -54AF on November 23. Total, "standard" DC-8 production included 240 passenger models plus 15 freighters and 39 convertibles.

Pan Am operated one DC-8-62, N1803 (ln 299/msn 45895) on an interchange service with Braniff in 1970-71.
(Author's Collection)

An unidentified DC-8-63CF of Flying Tigers wears a shark's mouth, which was removed shortly after delivery ceremonies.

SAS operated six DC-8-63s, including SE-DBH (ln 392/msn 45924). Now with Aer Turas as EI-CGO, it has flown more than 80,000 hours.

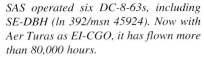

Air Afrique's DC-8-63CF TU-TCF (ln 531/msn 46135) is one of the few remaining unconverted model 63s. It now flies for ATI.

Air Congo became Air Zaire one year after DC-8-63CF 9Q-CLG (ln 540/msn 46151) was delivered in November 1970.

Danish charter operator Sterling Airways purchased DC-8-63 OY-SBK (ln 383/msn 45923) from SAS in 1984 and sold it back a year later. (Jeff Burch)

SAS bought this ex-Eastern DC-8-63PF (ln 503/msn 46097) for use by its charter subsidiary Scanair. The plane was re-registered LN-MOF. (Author's Collection)

Originally with KLM, Air Seychelles DC-8-63 S5-SIS (ln 533/msn 46141) now flies for Airborne Express as N824AX. (Author's Collection)

Later re-registered HS-TGY, Thai International DC-8-63 LN-MOY (ln 453/msn 46054) shows its origins. (Author's Collection)

Air Bahama leased DC-8-63CF TF-FLE (ln 489/msn 46101) from Flugleidir in 1977. (B. Sveinsson)

Air Canada's DC-8-63 C-FTIO (ln 451/msn 46076) was converted to a freighter and later received a CFM engine upgrade. (Author's Collection)

Independent carrier Air Siam operated this DC-8-63CF, N863F (ln 395/msn 46001) on lease in 1971-'72. (Author's Collection)

Wein Air Alaska operated freight services to the Lower 48 with DC-8-63CF N774FT (ln 454/msn 46087), on lease from Flying Tigers. (Author's Collection)

Above: Austrian Airlines ventured into the trans-Atlantic market during 1973 with DC-8-63CF OE-IBO (ln 464/msn 46088), leased from ONA. (Author's Collection) Below: Following conversion to a pure freighter, the same aircraft now serves with Emery as N865F. (via Eddy Gual)

DC-8 AWACS
DESIGN PROPOSAL

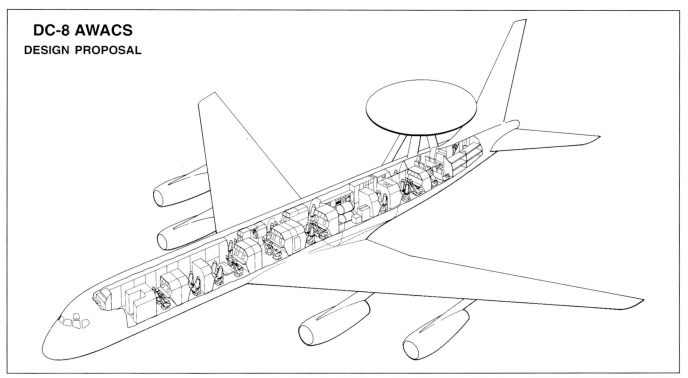

Right: *AWACS proposal full-size wooden fuse-lage and roto-dome shares floor space with a wide-body DC-10 cabin mock-up.*

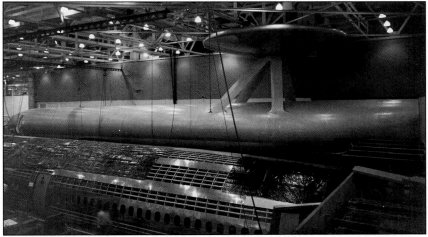

During 1968, the AWACS requirement surfaced again. This time the Douglas entry was based on the DC-8-62 airframe, equipped with the 35-foot-diameter roto-dome. A full size mock-up was erected, complete with roto-dome, and reviewed by the military in June 1969. The U.S. Air Force finally made a decision, and awarded the contract to Boeing, which was running out of work at the time.

Built as a DC-8-63, VIASA's YV-C-VIA (ln 421/msn 46042) was later converted to a -63F and now serves with Arrow Air as N345JW.

The End Of The Line

Few DC-8s were sold in the last three years of production, but four new customers came forward: African carrier Air Zaire; Atlantis, a West German charter operator, plus U.S. supplemental carriers World Airways and American Flyers (AFA). Fourteen orders were received in 1969: from Airlift, one -63CF; Air Zaire, two -63CFs; American Flyers, two -63CFs; Atlantis, one -63CF; Braniff, two -62s; JAL, one -62AF and four -61s; and SAS, one -63. In 1970, Atlantis bought two more model 63CFs and JAL added two -62s plus two -62CFs in December. Airlift ordered three model 63CFs, but canceled the order when the aircraft were almost complete. All were stored at Long Beach until bought by World Airways. Two DC-8-63s for Iberia were also stored for several months, awaiting financing. Last to be sold was a model 63 in April 1971, when Ship 556 was bought by SAS.

The company was anxious to close its DC-8 line in order to make way for DC-10 production, but the sales team made a final sweep around the airlines for last-minute orders before the deadline was reached. Sufficient raw material was on hand to build several more, but there were no takers. As luck would have it, Douglas received several inquiries several months later regarding re-opening the line, but it was too late; the decision was firm.

Although no new orders were being accepted, a substantial backlog of DC-8s still existed. The production rate was methodically decreased; 85 DC-8s came off the line in 1969, including ten model 62s for United, most of which were placed on Hawaii-East Coast routes. Eastern also received all six of its -63PFs. Production dropped sharply, to 33 in 1970.

DC-10 production was building up as the DC-8 line slowed to one a month in 1971 and ended with the final four in the first quarter of 1972. After delivery of the last aircraft to SAS on May 17, 1972, the manufacturing jigs were destroyed to make way for expanded DC-10 production and to avoid inventory taxes. The Series 60 was a great success; many of the 262 built are still in regular service today.

Total DC-8 revenue sales were $4.2 billion, but in view of the early cost over-runs and delayed deliveries, it is questionable as to whether the program was actually profitable. It was certainly a contributing factor in causing the merger with McDonnell. And, as with any aircraft program, a steady demand for spare parts remains long after the final aircraft is built. The DC-8's longevity has ensured a considerable income over the following years for Douglas and its suppliers. Forty-eight airlines bought DC-8s off the production lines, but many more were to operate it.

One of the few DC-8s operated by Egyptair, this DC-8-62 N772CA (ln 517/msn 46131) was sub-leased for Hajj flights in 1989.
(via Eddy Gual)

N993CF (ln 462/msn 46028), built as a model 62, was later converted to a -62F. (Author)

Balair acquired many aircraft from its parent company Swissair, including DC-8-62CF HB-IDH (ln 370/msn 45984).
(H. Oehninger)

All-cargo DC-8-62CF I-DIWQ (ln 361/msn 45961) began its career with Alitalia. Photographed at New York-JFK in January 1969. (Harry Sievers)

MGM Grand Air operated luxury service between Los Angeles and New York with three DC-8-62s, including N802MG (ln 516/msn 46098).
(Author's Collection)

DC-8-63CF N4868T (ln 519/msn 46091) of Transamerica (formerly Trans International) on approach to Oakland.
(Author's Collection)

Now part of the Airborne Express fleet as N822AX (ln 476/msn 46079) DC-8-63 EC-BQS initially served with Iberia and Aviaco.
(IAPS)

Above: Air India has leased many DC-8s, including -63CF TF-FLC (ln 479/msn 46049) from Icelandic in 1985-86. (Author's Collection)
Below: The same aircraft, converted to a pure freighter, now serves Burlington Air Express as N867BX. (Tim Williams)

World Airways bought six DC-8-63CFs, including N801WA (ln 534/msn 46133).
(Chuck Stewart)

Factory Deliveries

Model	10	20	30	40	50	50 AF	50 CF	61	61 CF	62	62 AF	62 CF	63	63 AF	63 CF	63 PF	Total
Aeromexico		1			6												7
Air Afrique					2		1								1		4
Air Canada				11	3		8	7					13				42
Air N.Z.					5												5
Air Zaire															2		2
Airlift Intl.							2								4		6
Alitalia				15						9		2					26
Am. Flyers															2		2
Atlantis															3		3
Braniff			4				1			6		1					12
CPA/CP Air				6	1								4				11
Capitol Intl.							3								4		7
Delta	6				15			13									34
Eastern		15			1			17								6	39
Finnair												3					3
Flying Tiger							2							7	10		19
Gaauda					1												1
Iberia					7		1						5		1		14
Japan A/L			5		10		2	9	10		5						41
KLM			7		9		3						11				30
National		3			6			2									11
Northwest			5														5
ONA							2								4		6
Philippine					2		1										3
Pan Am			19														19
Panair Braz.			2														2
SAS			7		2		1			7	1	2	6				26
Saturn									2								2
Seaboard							4								12		16
Swissair			3		1					5		2					11
TIA					1		2	3							7		13
Trans Carib.					2		4	3									9
United	22	15			13	15		30	10								185
Universal									2								2
UTA			5				2			4							11
VIASA					2								2				4
World															3		3
Total	**28**	**34**	**57**	**32**	**89**	**15**	**39**	**78**	**10**	**51**	**6**	**10**	**41**	**7**	**53**	**6**	**556**

Chapter VII
A New Lease On Life

DC-8 Conversions

As more modern and fuel-efficient aircraft entered service, older DC-8s were traded in against new equipment or sold off to smaller carriers. A good example is Pan Am, which phased out its DC-8 fleet by early 1969. Eastern cleared the earlier DC-8s from its inventory by January 1971, and even completed a profitable lease-purchase deal with JAL to dispose of seven model -61s, making way for TriStars deliveries. United eliminated its non-turbofan-powered aircraft by 1976, including 28 older DC-8s traded to Boeing as part of a 727-200 buy. In turn, many of the Douglas jets went to charter companies in Europe and also dribbled into the Latin American and African markets. However, a new industry was also spawned to convert some discarded passenger aircraft into freighters.

On average, most DC-8s being retired had far less than 30,000 flight hours in their log books, so were comparatively "young" airframes. The original water tank trials had demonstrated that these hours could easily be doubled, making the rework worthwhile. Douglas manufacturing techniques had kept corrosion to a minimum; usually found only in the galley and toilet areas. Cargo floor and door designs already existed, so the change was comparatively cheap and easy to complete. At the time, a used DC-8-20/30 could be bought for between $400,000 and $500,000, depending on the model,

Capitol DC-8-33 N900CL (ln 91/msn 45265) first flew with Pan Am. (Jeff Burch)

European charter airlines were primary customers for cast-off DC-8s:
Top: *Canafrica DC-8-61 EC-DZA (ln 436/msn 46032). (Author's Collection)*
Center: *Spantax DC-8-61 EC-EZE (ln 325/msn 45913). (Author's Collection)*
Bottom: *Sudflug DC-8-32 D-ADIM (ln 54/msn 45416). (Author)*

Another former Pan Am DC-8, is this reconfigured model 33F in cargo service with Zantop; N8240U (ln 44/msn 45257). (Jeff Burch)

hours and general condition. The door and floor modifications added another $500,000, including re-certification. To re-engine the aircraft and make structural changes for certification as a model 50F raised the total price to around $1.8 million, compared to a near new Jet Trader costing over $5 million.

Led by Charlotte Aircraft Corp. in 1974, several companies initiated simple conversions on a small scale by strengthening the cabin floors, installing the cargo doors and adding tie-downs and roller systems similar to the Jet Trader. All passenger amenities were removed and window panes were replaced by sheet metal. At least 25 DC-8-30s were modified to -32/33Fs, and nine Series 10s and 20s converted to the model 21F configuration.

There was so much demand for converted freighters that even Douglas set up a production line in March 1976 at its Tulsa, Oklahoma facility. Modification options included JT3D engine replacements and re-certifying the aircraft as a model 50F. An agreement was reached with aircraft broker F.B. Ayer and Associates to locate suitable candidate aircraft and assist in re-marketing after conversion. Two Series 43s were upgraded to -43F on a speculative basis in September. Initially intended for an Egyptian customer, the aircraft went to U.S. leasing companies and were operated by Aero Peru. DC-8-50s were also converted to freighters for ONA,

TransMeridian and IAS during the same time period. Three other -43s were brought up to the -54F standard, serving with Zantop and Airlift. Typically, aircraft down-time for a complete conversion was around 13 weeks.

UTA Industries in Paris converted two model 33s to 54Fs for the French Air Force plus one for TAE of Spain; Aeronavali in Italy also did some conversions. By the early 1980s, at least 17 DC-8-50s were re-worked into cargo aircraft, mostly in the United States, and are still in service today, averaging some 60,000 hours of flying time each.

By the early 1970s, the advent of the 747 and the large tri-jets began to make the narrow-bodied aircraft less attractive to the traveling public. Boeing began revamping the interiors of its 707, 727 and 737s to include enclosed overhead bins, cleaner ceilings, new sidewalls and better lighting, to give a more spacious look.

In 1972, agreements were reached for HeathTechna Corp. to manufacture DC-8 wide-body interior kits at its Kent, Washington factory and United Air Lines to install them in its fleet. The kits were also made available to other carriers. Changes were limited to the installation of new overhead bins and modification of ceiling panels and overhead lighting. In addition, United reduced a portion of the coach section to five-across seating, as part of a three-class layout. Earlier models of the DC-8 needed more work on the side

OB-R-1143 (ln 57/msn 45598) of Aero Peru is one of the few model 43s to have received a freighter conversion. It crashed near Mexico City on August 1, 1980. (Author's Collection)

Aeronaves de Mexico leased DC-8-63CF N4866T (ln 501/msn 46089) for three years from Trans International.
(Author's Collection)

DC-8-63CF D-ADIX (ln 527/msn 46137) of Atlantis, a German
charter company, which also took over Sudflug's fleet of DC-8-30s.

This DC-8-63PF originally flew for Eastern Airlines. N793AL (ln 503/msn 46097) was converted to a pure freighter prior to joining Arrow Air. It now serves with Airborne Express as N815AX.
(Author's Collection)

N8971U (ln 471/msn 46081) was the prototype Series 70, flown by Douglas crews for Cammacorp. It was later converted to an executive aircraft for ARAMCO and re-registered N728A.

panels, including the replacement of window curtains with pull-down blinds. The conversion cost was $120,000, compared to a 707 which ran more than $200,000.

Also in 1972, Douglas designers teamed up with Atlantic Aviation, Inc. to develop a similar wide-body interior. A 100-inch long mock-up was built at Long Beach to show potential customers the new look, featuring a lower, rounded ceiling, new side walls and window frames, fluorescent lights and enclosed overhead luggage racks. The venture was successful, and Japan Airlines became the first customer, with an order for 25 sets. Nine model 62s were modified for JAL by United at San Francisco, and the fleet of sixteen -61s were later re-worked at JAL's Tokyo-Haneda facility. All sets were built by Atlantic Aviation under license from Douglas. The program was completed by the end of 1975. Modification costs averaged about $700,000 per aircraft.

The DC-8 Seventy Series

By the early 1970s, noise generated by the first generation jets was becoming unacceptable, and it appeared by 1973 that the DC-8- 60s in particular, were in danger of being banned from major airports in North America. Various retrofit kits were being made available to comply with the current regulations, and ran about $770,000 for a DC-8. Even tougher rules appeared to be inevitable in the future.

At the request of several major U.S. airlines, Douglas began looking at ways to reduce engine noise. By January 1975, it had identified several solutions. The first was a new version of the JT3B power plant, which would need about three years to develop. It would be accompanied by a nacelle treated with noise-absorbing material. The estimated $6 million cost effectively restricted such a program to the DC-8-61 and -63.

A second promising alternative was to install de-rated CF-6s, used on the DC-10, at a cost of over $10 million per

ship set, but the engines were considered too powerful and expensive at the time.

General Electric, makers of the CF-6, held meetings with a number of airlines in July 1975, proposing to re-engine DC-8s and Boeing 707s with the new 22,000-pound thrust CFM-56 turbofan, but nothing came of the idea. The new noise regulations were still not clearly spelled out, and airlines preferred to wait until the rules were clear.

Also in question was who would pay for the costs of meeting new regulations, either in the form of modifications or even new replacement aircraft. There were proposals circulating in Congress to institute an additional ticket tax to pay a percentage of the cost, but none came to fruition. In March 1977, it was stipulated that all aircraft weighing in excess of 75,000 pounds must meet Federal Air Regulation (FAR) Part 36, Stage 3 by January 1, 1985. As predicted, this rule mandated even more stringent noise restrictions.

A new company, Cammacorp, was formed in 1977 by Jackson R. McGowen, by then retired from Douglas Aircraft. Staffed almost entirely by other recently retired Douglas executives, it was set up to act as a contractor for any type of DC-8 retrofitting projects. The new company immediately started talks with General Electric and Societe Nationale d'Etude et de Construction de Moteurs d'Avation-SNECMA, its European partner in the CFM-56 program, and shortly afterwards, joint studies were initiated. Each engine manufacturer was to provide half of any engines sold.

McDonnell Douglas Corp. (MDC) was not particularly anxious to manage such a program since it was busy on the DC-10, starting to look at the MD-80 and also working hard on the proposed DC-X-200 wide-body twin-jet. But in May 1977, MDC announced that it was in talks with two airlines, again proposing to re-engine the DC-8. This time, the candidates were a 24,000-pound thrust CFM-56-1, de-rated to 22,000 pounds, and the new Pratt & Whitney 19,000-pound-thrust JT8D-209, which was destined to power the DC-9-80 series. (MDC was already flight-testing a DC-9-31, known as

Geneva-based SATA bought DC-8-63CF HB-IDS (ln 389/msn 45968) from Flying Tigers in 1975 and resold it to the same company three years later.
(Author's Collection)

Three days after delivery, CP Air leased DC-8-63 CF-CPS (ln 334/msn 45929) to Flying Tigers for one year. It was re-registered N624FT.
(Author)

DC-8-63 EC-BQS (ln 476/msn 46079) rests at Iberia's Barajas Airport base in Madrid; July 1977. (Author)

DC-8-71 (N822E ln 288/msn 45907) in the colors of Delta, first airline to place a Series 70 example into revenue service.
(Author's Collection)

the "Refan DC-9," powered by the JT8D-204, forerunner of the -209). The JT8D entry appeared to be the simplest solution as it could be attached to the existing model 62/63 pylons and retain the JT3B's thrust reversers. However, installing it on the model 61 would require -63 pylons, a more complex modification.

The CFM-56-1 required totally new pylons, but its advantages included a substantially reduced fuel burn, shorter field length requirements, higher initial cruise altitude, and less noise. The CFM was about 135 pounds lighter, but the new pylons would each exceed existing examples by 500 pounds. The model that stood to gain the biggest performance improvement was the -61, due to elimination of the over-wing portion of the pylons.

Delta was first to admit looking at the DC-8 re-engine proposal. In May 1978, it was struggling with the decision for a new generation 200-seat aircraft, and the model 61s were already the right size. The JT8D-powered DC-8 appeared to be Delta's engine of choice at the time, but the front runner proposal was the proposed short-body Lockheed "TriStar 400" with de-rated engines. By year's end, United and Flying Tigers had joined Delta in a joint study of the re-engine options. At the same time, it was announced that Pratt & Whitney would self-manage any JT8D re-engine program,

while CFM International had reached agreement with Cammacorp to manage its program and also be the sales organization for the CFM-56. MDC provided data and engineering support to both parties, but avoided favoring either of the candidates. The company also offered to contract for all the engineering, flight testing and certification work.

The competition heated up in February 1979, when Pratt & Whitney announced that it was prepared to go ahead with the production of JT8D-209s or 20,000-pound thrust JT8D-217s, upon receipt of an order for 75 DC-8 conversions. The Pratt & Whitney engines were priced at $980,000 each, compared to the CFM's $1.5 million per unit. Cammacorp also indicated that 75 orders would be the start-up requirement.

United's announcement on March 29 that it had placed a $400 million order to re-engine its 29-ship DC-8-61 fleet with CFM-56-1 engines was a surprise. United's engineering staff had initially favored the JT8D, but was asked by Flying Tigers to take a second look. Tigers' concern was that engine "cut-back" procedures, requiring reduction of power just after takeoff, might be required at some airports to meet local noise requirements, particularly at night when it did a lot of flying. It was also argued that long-term fuel savings would offset the CFM's higher purchase price. By mid-April, Flying Tigers had contracted with Cammacorp for the conversion of

ADVANTAGES OF NEW ENGINES OVER THE JT3D-3B AND JT3D-7								
	DC-8-61		**DC-8-62**		**DC-8-63**		**DC-8-63F**	
ENGINE	JT8D-209	CFM-56	JT8D-209	CFM-56	JT8D-209	CFM-56	JT8D-209	CFM-56
Reduction in fuel burn (%) (3,000 nmi.)	11.70	21.60	7.40	12.80	6.40	13.70	6.30	12.60
Range increase (n.mi)	500	800	440	800	400	680	300	550
Take-off field length (ft)	+75	-800	+75	-700	+700	-850	+700	-850
Noise reduction (Cum Epndb)	30.60	42.50	29.40	41.20	29.60	40.40	29.60	40.40

United's DC-8-71 N8097U (ln 459/msn 46064) pauses before takeoff at San Francisco International. UAL was one of the largest operators of stretched DC-8s. (Author's Collection)

its seven model 63CFs and two -61CFs; the carrier's remaining DC-8s were leased. After Delta contracted for thirteen model 61 upgrades, McGowen announced that letters of intent for a total of 78 aircraft from seven airlines were in hand, and the program was formally launched. The basic re-engine cost was about $12 million per aircraft.

Cammacorp then entered into agreement with MDC for its Long Beach division to provide all the engineering support; actual conversion work would be undertaken at the Tulsa plant. Delta decided to have just one aircraft converted at Tulsa, with the rest done in-house at Atlanta, using kits purchased from Cammacorp. This allowed the airline to incorporate many other planned changes and scheduled maintenance during the down-time. The first flight was targeted for mid-1981.

By the end of May 1979, Grumman Aerospace had been contracted to manufacture the engine nacelles and pylons, which were designed to be interchangeable with the four wing stations, unlike the earlier pylons which were "handed" (left or right) due to their aerodynamic contouring. The first aircraft to undergo conversion was a DC-8-61, N8093U of United, that was delivered to Tulsa in October 1980. At the time of this delivery, it was announced that the converted DC-8-61, -62, and -63 models would be re-designated as DC-8-71, -72 and -73 respectively.

More contracts were signed by the end of the year with Spantax for 3, Cargolux for 3, and Trans-America Airlines for 7, bringing total firm orders to 63, plus 24 options and 22 letters of intent.

New orders continued to come in during 1981. Tigers' lessors agreed to nine more conversions, including five model 61CFs owned by Trans- America. The French Air Force (L'Armee de l'Air) signed for a DC-8-62CF to be converted by UTA with the kits provided by Cammacorp, and took an option on a second aircraft. Air Canada added six -73AFs while Capitol Airlines and Overseas National Airways (ONA) contracted for two -71CFs each; Capitol later increased the order to four in 1982. A Swiss company, Jet Aviation, bought a model 63 for conversion to an executive

jet -73 for a Middle East customer. In March, Cammacorp acquired a DC-8-62 from United for conversion to an executive configured -72 for the Arab American Company (ARAMCO), anticipating a type certificate for that model by March 1982.

The first Flying Tigers model 63 arrived at Tulsa in April 1981. The target date for model 73 certification was January 1982. In addition to the engine change, other modifications included the addition of an auxiliary power unit and removal of the four turbo-compressors in the nose, used for cabin pressurization and air conditioning. They would be replaced with a pair of light-weight air cycle machines. This arrangement eliminated the need for nose intakes, but added exhaust vents below the cockpit.

As work progressed on the first model 61, it became apparent that the original goal of May 1981 for the maiden flight could not be met. It had been hoped to have the aircraft available at the Paris Air Show in June, but FAA and company inspections took longer than anticipated, so the first flight was finally made on August 15. Piloted by an MDC crew, the aircraft was aloft over five hours and landed at the Douglas test facility at Yuma, Arizona, where most of the testing was done. The DC-8-72 joined the test program in December, and the model 73 started flying in March 1982. It was used mainly for airport noise measurements as the first two aircraft had almost completed the required certification flights. Delta began modifying model 61s on February 1, aiming to put the aircraft back in revenue service by April. UTA was also completing its first conversion, and contracted to do two more for the Armee de L'Air.

The FAA awarded the DC-8-71 type certificate on April 13, 1981; the models 72 and 73 followed a month later. Flight testing was completed in 725 hours and 437 flights. United took delivery of its first model 71, N8092U, on May 10, and began service on May 16, between San Francisco and Portland, Oregon. However, Delta was first with revenue -71 service, on April 24, flying from Atlanta to Savannah. Trans-America started -73 flights on June 2, with scheduled nonstop service from Oakland to Shannon, Ireland, operating in a

254-seat configuration with low-cost unrestricted fares for tourists.

By the end of September, 16 of the 97 conversions on firm order had been completed; Cammacorp was getting back to its promised schedule. Its order book stood as follows:

Customer	Type	Order	Rec'd
Air Canada	73	6	
ARAMCO	72	1	1
Capitol	71	2	
Delta	71	13	4
Flying Tigers	73/71	18	1
French A.F.	72	3	1
Govt. Gabon	73CF	1	1
Handling Air	73	1	1
Int'l. Air Leases	71CF	3	
Jet Aviation	71	1	1
ONA	71CF	2	1
Spantax	71	3	
Trans America	73	12	
United	71	29	5
Unannounced	?	2	
Total		**97**	**16**

At the end of a sales tour to England and the Middle East, Cammacorp's model 72 made a nonstop 8,300-mile flight from Cairo to Los Angeles in 15 hours, 46 minutes on April 3, 1983, piloted by former Douglas test pilot Don Mullin. On arrival, the aircraft still had fuel on board for another 1,000 miles of flying.

At the first anniversary of commercial operation, 38 "Super 70s" had been delivered. United was averaging 16 hours a day with some aircraft on the Denver-Hawaii service. A few teething problems emerged with the CFM-56-1, engine starters and dust clogging the high-pressure turbine cooling blade circuits. The starter problem was soon fixed, and to solve the dust ingestion the Douglas "blowaway" system was tested on a Delta model 71. However, internal modifications proved to be more efficient, and were incorporated instead.

Despite the early problems, dispatch reliability was running at 99.86 percent. CFM continued to improve the engine, and offered the CFM-56-2 which had a further 6.2 percent reduction in fuel burn. Retrofit kits were also made available.

Series 70 conversion orders fluctuated during the remainder of the program. Cancellations were usually due to the demise of airlines (such as Spantax), while additions came from UPS, Emery Worldwide, German Cargo, and several smaller carriers. By early 1986, final order figures stood at 110. Of these, MDC-Tulsa handled 44 conversions and Delta completed 48, while Air Canada and UTA Industries undertook nine each. The last to be produced was a DC-8-72 for NASA, which replaced Galileo II, a CV-990 destroyed by fire in 1985.

More stretched DC-8s might well have been re-engined, were it not for the U.S. government's extension of the requirement for all jet aircraft to meet FAR 36, Part 2 noise restrictions. The compliance date was moved from 1983 to January 1, 1986, with Stage 3 required by January 1, 2000. The FAA had been inundated with requests for variances, especially by Latin American carriers.

The availability of cheaper hush-kits, which brought the aircraft up to FAR 36, Part 2 standards, was also a big factor; falling fuel prices lessened the advantages of the CFM-56's improved burn rate. By the time the last model 70s were being delivered, the conversion price had escalated to around $15 million and few suitable airframes were available.

In mid-1986, Cammacorp began winding down as planned, having ensured that warranties and spares would be covered by its sub-contractors. The venture was deemed a profitable experience for all parties.

Cammacorp made one other major improvement to the DC-8, which was later adopted up by other companies. In April 1984, an FAA supplemental type certificate (STC) was awarded for a glass-cockpit version of the DC-8-72. The

Originally DC-8-62 N8972U with United, line number 473 (msn 46084) also flew with Air Jamaica as 6Y-JII prior to being purchased by Cammacorp in December 1982. Upgraded to a model 72 the following month N2547R is seen at the Paris Air Show in June 1983, wearing exhibition number 62. *(Michel Ramel)*

Built as a DC-8-63, CF-TIQ (ln 508/msn 46123) was converted to an all-cargo configuration and later upgraded to a -73F.
(via Eddy Gual)

company's demonstrator aircraft was converted by installing a Collins Electronic Flight Instrument System (EFIS) and new Collins Air Data System, Honeywell Laser Navigation system and color radar. It was the first real DC-8 cockpit upgrade.

The final breakdown of DC-8-70 Series conversions is shown in the table at right.

AIRLINE	71	72	73
Air Canada			6 (F)
Al Nasar			1
ARAMCO		1	
Delta	13		
Brightstar		1	
Emery Worldwide			7 (F)
French Air Force		3 CF	
Evergreen Int'l.			1
Gabon Govt.			1
German Cargo			5 (F)
Handling Air			1
Icelandair			1
NASA		1	
Minerve	1		
Oman Royal Flt.			1
ONA			2 (CF)
Trans America			7 (CF)
United	29		
UPS	10 (F)		18 (F)
TOTAL	**53**	**7**	**50**

Opposite Page: Series 70 conversions included:

Above: *Ex-Eastern DC-8-63PF N8760*
(ln 468/msn 46074), now with UPS as N874UP.
(Author's Collection)
Center: *Ex-Flying Tigers -63CF N792FT*
(ln 444/msn 46046) currently flown by Emery Worldwide.
(via Eddy Gual)
Bottom: *Ex-Seaboard World -63CF N8641 (ln 490/msn 46106),*
operated by German Cargo as D-ADUC. (via Eddy Gual)

An optical illusion! Formerly a DC-8-63 with CP Air, N29180 (ln 497/msn 46095) had just been upgraded to model 73F standards, following purchase by Cammacorp. The Canadian carrier never operated Series 70 DC-8s. *(Author's Collection)*

Former United DC-8-61s converted to model 71 freighters:
N824BX (ln 339/msn 45946) – Burlington Air Express. (Roy Lock)
N8099U (ln 462/msn 46066) – Flagship Express. (Mike Rathke)
The same aircraft, later with Tampa Colombia as HK-3785X. (Author)
N870SJ (ln 448/msn 46039) – Mexicana Cargo. (Author's Collection)

DC-8-71F CC-CAX (ln 343/msn 45970), leased to FastAir by GPA. (Author)

Primarily a Boeing operator, Lan Chile's colors look smart on DC-8-71F CC-CDS (ln 397/msn 45996). (Author's Collection)

Flying Tigers leased DC-8-73CF N4865T (ln 485/msn 46073) from September 1988 until the company was acquired by Federal Express. (Author's Collection)

DHL Worldwide Express DC-8-73F N803DH (ln 508/msn 46123) first flew for Air Canada.
(via Eddy Gual)

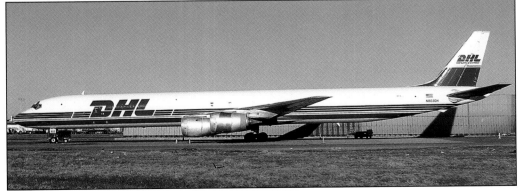

Series 70 conversions:
F-GDRM (ln 457/msn 46063) – Aire d'Evasions. (via Eddy Gual)
D-ADUE (ln 432/msn 46044) – Lufthansa Cargo. (Author's Collection)
N816EV (ln 375/msn 45990) – TNT. (via Eddy Gual)

ADC used ex-Swissair DC-8-62 (ln 470/msn 46077) for its hush-kitting flight-test program. (Seymour Hills)

More Changes

As the scheduled passenger airlines began retiring DC-8-50s and -60s, there was an insatiable demand for the types from freight and small package carriers. Aeronavali, the Venice, Italy-based aircraft overhaul company, was quick to identify a market for converting the surplus aircraft into freighters, particularly the Series 60s. In late 1983, Air Canada became the first customer for conversion of its DC-8-63s to -63Fs. UPS became a major customer in 1985; thirteen ex-Delta DC-8-71s plus three other model 73s were converted to the all-cargo layout over a five-year period. Delta's last -71 revenue flight was flown between Baltimore and Atlanta on May 1, 1989, closing out nearly 30 years of DC-8 operations by the airline.

An even larger contract was signed with Guinness Peat Aviation (GPA), an Irish leasing company. GPA had bought all 29 of United's model 71s (plus spares and related equipment) in early 1990 for $500 million. The aircraft were then leased back to United for various periods to match the carrier's integration of new aircraft. Between 1990 and 1994, twenty-six -71s were submitted to Aeronavali for model 71F conversion.

Airborne Express built up a large fleet of DC-8s, particularly model 62s and 63s, but opted not to install cargo doors and flooring, instead simply stripping out the passenger related interior fixtures. However, to reduce maintenance and simplify' operations, most have had major cockpit upgrades, including installation of the Electronic Flight Instrument System (EFIS). Airborne announced that the enhancements helped dispatch reliability jump to over 99 percent, as 34 percent of previous delays had been due to cockpit navigation and avionics problems, now eliminated by EFIS. UPS progressively updated its DC-8 fleet in a similar manner.

The remaining DC-8s not re-equipped with CFM-56s were still required to meet FAR 36, Part 2, which gave vendors an opportunity to develop hush-kits for the JT3Bs. Five companies produced sound-proofed nacelle designs, with three concentrating on the model 62 and 63 long-duct nacelles. The most successful was the Aeronautic Development Corp. (ADC), based in Jersey, Channel Islands. Formed in 1983, ADC did no actual work, but sub-contracted out the design, manufacture and testing to several well-established companies including Rohr Industries, which designed and built the original nacelles.

Design work began in 1983, followed by flight testing of a DC-8-63CF to establish base-line noise levels in February 1984. The actual testing of new nacelles was done on an ex-Swissair DC-8-62. After some preliminary flights with "boiler plate" hush-kits, testing of fully treated nacelles took place between February and June 1985. Flight Test Systems carried out the work at the FAA's Fresno, California facility.

An STC was issued for the JT3D-3B engine in June 1984, followed by the JT3D-7 in July. The reduced noise levels were achieved by lengthening the nose dome and front cowling by 12 inches, and replacing the existing fan ducts with new examples lined with "DynaRohr" acoustically treated panels. Fifty-five ship sets were built. Some operators,

Quiet Nacelle Corp. acquired DC-8-55JT N801FB (ln 346/msn 45965) for JT3D hush-kit certification testing.   (Author's Collection)

Former Braniff DC-8-62 N801BN (ln 458/msn 46082) used by Nacelle Corp. for DC-8-62 hush-kit development. (Author's Collection)

Ex-United DC-8-61s of GPA Group, leased after conversion as follows:
Above: Model 71F EI-TLD (ln 277/msn 45812) – Translift Airways. (via Eddy Gual)
Below: Model 71F PP-SOQ (ln 317/msn 45941) – VASP. (Jeff S. Johnson)
Opposite Page Top: Model 71 EI-BZU (ln 387/msn 45994) – Kenya Airways. (Author's Collection)
Opposite Page Bottom: Model 71F SE-DLM (ln 356/msn 45971) – Time Air Sweden. (Author's Collection)

including SAS, installed the kits in-house, but Wardair-Canada also modified a number of aircraft for customers including Icelandair, Emery and Aer Turas.

Quiet Nacelle Corp. of Waco, Texas was another company to achieve success in marketing a DC-8-62/63 hush-kit, using a similar approach to that taken by ADC, except that the nose cowl and center body were not extended, but given double layers of acoustic lining. Considerable use of honey-comb panels, made from composite material, was used in the design. Again, much of the work was sub-contracted, and the manufacturing completed by Nordam in Tulsa, Oklahoma. Another model 62, called "the Quiet DC-8," flew the test program at Fresno, California, in August 1985. Initial flights utilized JT3D-3B engines, followed shortly by a second series with JT3D-7s.

In early October, Nacelle Corp. received its STC for the JT3-3B modification, followed by the JT3D-7's approval in late November. Seven airlines bought 28 kits which were distributed and supported by PageAvjet of Orlando, Florida. In June 1987, Nacelle Corp. also received approval to install hush-kits on the DC-8-50s and -61s, using a Jet Trader for the flight testing. Noise reduction was achieved by acoustically treating the engine center body, plus its inlet and exhaust ducts. A ship set cost around $2.5 million. Some landing-weight restrictions were initially imposed, but these were raised in January 1988, when a new STC restored 8,000 pounds to the maximum landing weight. Approval was also obtained to use the hush-kit on the JT3B-powered DC-8-50s

not fitted with the 4-percent-leading-edge modification. Ironically, the model 62 used in the test program was subsequently converted to a -72 for NASA.

Snow Aviation was also a successful developer of hush-kits for short- and long-duct nacelles; its customers including Worldways Canada.

Stage 3 Partners was formed in September 1988 to improve existing hush-kits for model 62s and 63s to meet FAR 36, Stage 3 regulations. It was a joint venture, combining ADC and The Quiet Nacelle Corp., and merged their data, technology and resources. Engine runs in a test cell started shortly after the announcement, with the first test flights taking place in early 1989. Approval was obtained later that year, and production conversions commenced in early 1990.

A late starter in the hush-kit business was Burbank Aeronautical Corp., which commenced test flights of its Stage 2 hush kit for the JT3B-powered model 50s and 61s in 1987. Flight testing was completed by October 1987, and the STC was approved in April 1988. This kit differed from the others in that it was an all-metal design, and substantially cheaper, costing around $1.65 million per ship set, including installation. Airborne Express was the major customer for the version. In July 1990, it was upgraded to FAR 36, Stage 3 level.

UAS Engineering, a New York company, offered a new version of a hush-kit system in September 1990. It included an extended nose cone, for the DC-8-50 series.

TransContinental DC-8-63 N820TC (ln 377/msn 45999) was later converted to a pure freighter and is currently with ATI as N788L.
(Rick Neibert)

Hawaiian Airlines operated DC-8-62 N8973U (ln 481/msn 46085) until DC-10s took over the carrier's long-haul routes. (Author)

An ex-United DC-8-62, N8974U (ln 487/msn 46110) appears in the old colors of Rich International. (via Eddy Gual)

Originally delivered to KLM as a DC-8-63, EI-CAK (ln 500/msn 46121) went on to haul cargo for Aer Turas. (Malcolm Nason)

N790AL (ln 496/msn 46093) of Challenge Air Cargo, is an example of a former Eastern model 63PF after conversion.
(via Eddy Gual)

One of many DC-8s flown by Arrow Air, DC-8-62F N8968U (ln 465/msn 46069) in new colors. (Author)

Chapter VIII

Non-Airline Operators

The Navy's EC-24 Bureau number 163050 (ln 352/msn 45881). (Bruce Trombecki)

Though Douglas was unsuccessful at placing DC-8s with the U.S. military, two aircraft were subsequently purchased by the government via the second-hand market. The first was an ex-United DC-8-54F, initially sold to Electrospace Systems, Inc. in November 1984. It underwent an extensive fitting of electronic counter-measure and counter-counter-measure equipment before being operated on behalf of the U.S. Navy by the Douglas facility in Tulsa, alongside two NKC-135As. It was assigned to the Fleet Electronic Warfare Support Group to provide specialized electronic warfare training. The aircraft was bought by the Navy in June 1987 and designated as an EC-24. Currently based in Waco, Texas, the aircraft is now maintained under contract by Chrysler Corp.

NASA acquired a DC-8-62 from Cammacorp in February 1986 and had it converted to a model 72 by Delta shortly thereafter. It was bought to replace the CV-990 which was written off in a takeoff accident at March AFB, California in July 1985. Based at the Ames Research Center, Moffett Field, near San Francisco, it carries research scientists and a large suite of test equipment on world-wide missions, using its ability to stay aloft for over 15 hours. Used primarily for upper atmosphere research, specialized missions include the study of ozone layer depletion at the North and South Poles.

The French Armee de L'Air has operated seven DC-8s in a variety of roles. One model 33 was bought from UAT in 1973 and modified as an electronic intelligence (ELINT) platform. It was re-engined with JT3Ds in 1980 and converted to a model 53. Operated by Escadron Electronique 51, it is being replaced by a newer DC-8 transferred from the other unit, Escadre de Transport 3/60, which currently operates as VIP transports three ex-Finnair DC-8-62CFs converted to model 72CFs, plus a DC-8-55CF. Based near Paris, the DC-8s also support French military activities in the South Pacific. Two other model 55CFs served for many years before being replaced by the -72s.

Other military DC-8 operators have included the Royal Thai Air Force, which flew three ex-Thai Airways -62CFs between 1985 and 1989. The Spanish Air Force, Ejercito del Aire Español, operated two ex-Iberia model 52s as VIP transports between 1978 and 1988. Swissair sold two DC-8-62s to the Peruvian Air Force, one in 1969 and one in 1981; both still remain in service with that air arm.

The Republics of Togo and Gabon each operated ex-UTA DC-8-50s as presidential transports for many years. Gabon replaced its aircraft with a DC-8-63CF in 1974 and had it converted to a model 73 in 1982, though it has been in storage since a takeoff incident in March 1993. The Omani government acquired a DC-8-63CF from World Airways in June 1981, converted it to a -73 in 1982, and operated it until 1993. Saudi Arabia's large fleet of government-owned executive jets includes a DC-8-72 bought in 1987. Many other DC-8s have been "commandeered" from flag carriers to

NASA DC-8-72 N717NA (ln 458/msn 46082) was built for Alitalia (I-DIWK) and later used for hush-kit trials by Nacelle Corp. – see Page 104. (via A. Pearcy)

Other military operators:
Top: *Fuerza Aerea Del Peru 370, DC-8-62CF (ln 475/msn 46078). (Author's Collection)*
Middle: *Royal Thai Air Force 60112, DC-8-62CF (ln 335/msn 45922). (Gary Vincent)*
Bottom: *Fuerza Aerea Española T.15-1/401-30, DC-8-52 (ln 258/msn 45814). (Jeff Burch)*

transport their nation's leaders and entourage when required. DC-8s have also been converted to corporate jets for large companies. Two model 62s and one -72 are currently operated on the Bermudan register for corporate customers, including one for an Australian and another for a Middle East company. The DC-8-72 was operated for awhile by ARAMCO, then given to Sheik Yamani. One DC-8-63PF was also converted, owned and operated by Handling Air on behalf of Sheik Adnan Khashoggi. This particular aircraft was sumptuously fitted out with liberal use of gold in its fittings. Even the carpets were woven from gold thread. The aircraft was sold to the Bank of Saudi Arabia, and then to Kalitta Air Services, where its ornate interior was removed for conversion to cargo service as N809CK.

Probably the most bizarre use of a DC-8 was in the summer of 1976 when an anonymous individual, identifying himself as the "Human Fly," flew at the California National Air Races, standing up on the upper fuselage of an ex-JAL DC-8-33. The idea was generated by the rider, who appeared at the airfield with a mask on his face. A typical wing-walker pylon and stirrups had been fastened to the fuselage crown to hold him in place. The aircraft, flown by Clay Lacy, made a few low-speed passes in front of the crowd. Afterwards the rider quickly disappeared, vowing that he would never repeat the experience and looking distinctly worse for having done it once! Apparently the air pressure on his body had made it difficult for him to breathe.

A more practical use was made of the fourth DC-8 built. It was converted to an mobile eye surgery plus training school and put into service in 1982. Donated to Project Orbis, a non-profit group dedicated to teaching eye surgery to doctors in over 70 under-developed countries, it roamed around Africa and Asia for eight years before being given to a Chinese museum in Beijing. The aircraft was given to the foundation by United, with conversion and operating funding received from several individuals. Staffed by groups of volunteers, the aircraft would be parked for a period and used as a clinic. Over 18,000 operations were carried out, and 28,000 doctors

Two ex-United DC-8-62s converted to model 72s for Middle East customers:
Above: VR-BJR (ln 455/msn 46067) – Al Nassr Ltd. (Roy Lock)
Below: HZ-MS11 (ln 473/msn 46084) – Saudi Arabian government Royal Flight. (Author's Collection)

The Government of Oman's DC-8-73CF A40-HMQ (ln 538/msn 46149). (Author's Collection)

and nurses received training aboard the DC-8 until it was replaced by a DC-10-10, equipped with more extensive, updated equipment and training aids.

Only two other DC-8s have been donated to museums. In 1984, United gave a DC-8-52 to Los Angeles Museum of Science and Industry. The wings were sawed off to allow it to be taken to its display site, then re-attached. The second museum DC-8 is a former Japan Airlines -61, which was damaged beyond economical repair while landing at Shanghai in 1982. It has been rebuilt to display standards and is now on show at a Shanghai museum, wearing a non-standard paint scheme.

Several DC-8s have been donated to airport fire services for rescue training, and Air Canada gave a model 53 to the Royal Canadian Mounted Police to use as a hostage rescue trainer. In Purmerend, Holland, an ex-Air Afrique DC-8 was converted to a restaurant in 1985. Several cockpit sections also survive.

DC-8s have appeared many times on the silver screen and in TV commercials. Perhaps the most unusual temporary paint job was applied to a DC-8 owned by American Jet Industries at Van Nuys, California, in 1977. It was made up to represent Air Force One, the presidential transport. More recently, two DC-8s, parked at Mojave, California, were painted in camouflage for a commercial.

In the late 1960s and early 1970s, there was a proliferation of travel clubs throughout the United States. Most acquired Electras, DC-7s or Constellations as club vehicles, with each member being a shareholder. Some managed to exist for a number of years, but most fell by the wayside quite quickly. With the availability of early model DC-8s and Boeing 720s at low prices, several clubs ventured into the jet market. Points of Call Canada operated a DC-8. There was even an ill-fated attempt to launch a transcontinental "hippy" airline, Freelandia Travel Club, in 1973 with an ex-National DC-8-21, which was to offer very low fares to the free-spirited members. Though the aircraft was painted up, it never made a flight due to lack of funds and some reluctance on the part of the FAA to allow its operation. Several resort and casino operators also transitioned from piston-engine transports to jets, such as the McCulloch Corp., which changed from Constellations to DC-8s to feed its resort in Nevada.

The "Human Fly" rides atop ex-JAL DC-8-33 N420AJ (ln 81/msn 45419) during the air races at Mojave, California, on June 19, 1976. (Harry Gann)

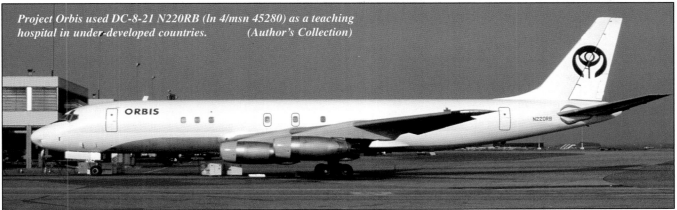

Project Orbis used DC-8-21 N220RB (ln 4/msn 45280) as a teaching hospital in under-developed countries.   (Author's Collection)

Above: *United's DC-8-52 N8066U (ln 257/msn 45850), City of Los Angeles, preserved at the Museum of Science and Industry, next to the L.A. Coliseum.   (via Eddy Gual)*

Left: *Offered for sale at $250,000 is the former Air Afrique DC-8-53 TU-TCB (ln 196/msn 45671), in use as a restaurant at Purmerend, Holland.   (Henk Geerlings)*

DC-8-33 (F) N421AJ (ln 113/msn 45421) camouflage painted for an American Airlines television commercial in August 1987. (Harry Gann) **Inset:** *Mystery DC-8 probably owned by American Jet International, dressed up as Air Force One for a movie; at Van Nuys, California, February 1977. (John Wegg)*

Freelandia's DC-8-31 N6571C (ln 38/msn 45391) at Los Angeles International in January 1974. (Author's Collection)

Ex-Eastern DC-8-21 N8609 (ln 99/msn 45430) while with the short-lived travel club Air Caledonia. (Author's Collection)

Concord International DC-8-31F N8207U (ln 64/msn 45275) originally served with Panagra as N8275H.
(Bruce Drum)

Eastern DC-8-21 N8160 (ln 103/msn 45431) displays an experimental livery at New York-JFK in November 1964. *(Harry Sievers)*

Wearing the classic Sun King color scheme, National DC-8-32 N7184C (ln 115/msn 45606) on approach to L.A. International in April 1968.
(Author)

N8005U (ln 10/msn 45282), a DC-8-11 converted to a -21, served its entire working life in the Friendly Skies of United. It is seen at New York-JFK in June 1975, three years before being traded to Boeing and reduced to spares. *(Harry Sievers)*

Chapter IX
Safety

DC-8-73CF TR-LTZ (ln 446/msn 46053) has been stored since its attempted takeoff from a taxiway at Frankfurt in September 1982.
(Author's Collection)

As with all commercial transport aircraft, the DC-8 has had its fair share of accidents and incidents. At least three airlines – UTA, Cubana and Swissair – lost examples to terrorist bombs. Fortunately, the Swissair aircraft was destroyed on the ground, with no loss of life. Several have been written off after fires started while on the ground, either during refueling or in hangar fires.

Two were involved in mid-air collisions. A United DC-8 struck a TWA 1049 Constellation over Brooklyn, New York on December 16, 1960, with disastrous results, both in the air and on the ground. The other incident was more fortuitous, for the crew and passengers of a Cubana DC-8-43 which collided with a Cubana An-24 on March 18, 1976 just after take-off from Havana. The DC-8 lost some 16 feet of an outer wing, but the crew were able to maintain control and land safely at Havana. However, the aircraft was declared a write-off.

In the early years of service, two accidents were attributable to control problems, both being suspected as horizontal tail trim compensator mechanical malfunctions. The first was a Trans-Canada Airlines Jet Trader which crashed on the evening of November 23, 1963, shortly after take off from Dorval, Montreal. The "most probable cause" was thought to be that the aircraft's pitch trim compensator had incorrectly trimmed the aircraft nose high. In an effort to offset this, the pilot had trimmed the horizontal stabilizer to a full nose-down position. As speed built up, the crew were unable to pull the aircraft out of an ever steepening dive due to the pressures on the control surfaces.

A similar incident took place near New Orleans on February 25, 1964, when an Eastern Air Lines DC-8-21 dove into Lake Pontchartrain shortly after takeoff. Again, the horizontal stabilizer was found to have been trimmed in a fully nose-down position. It was believed that the aircraft may have encountered wind shear and, during the attempts to pull the aircraft out of the ensuing dive, a chain drive failed. Again, the problem arose at an altitude too low for the crew to recover. At the time, the pitch trim compensator, which stops the aircraft from naturally nosing down, known as "tucking under," at high speeds, was inoperative, so the aircraft was flying under a speed restriction.

Approximately one-third of all DC-8 accidents have occurred while approaching an airport or in the final landing phase. Several were off course and hit high ground, while others undershot and hit approach lights or other obstructions.

Probably the most remarkable DC-8 incident took place at San Francisco on November 22, 1968, when a four-month old Japan Air Lines DC-8-62, JA8032, landed in San Francisco Bay, three miles short of the runway. With gear and flaps down, the aircraft landed in about 9 feet of water and came to a rapid stop. It remained completely intact, and everyone was rescued. There were no serious injuries and little panic. The weather was just above the airport minimums, with some fog, a 300-foot ceiling, and forward visibility of three-quarters of a mile. The experienced Japanese captain, assisted by two American crew members, stated that the decision height of 211 feet had been set on the radio altimeter but, when he looked up as the instrument flashed, they were

Eastern's DC-8-21 N8607 (ln 61/msn 45428) crashed into Lake Pontchartrain on February 25, 1964. (Clay Jansson)

DC-8-51 XA-NUS (ln 162/msn 45633) of Aeronaves de Mexico, seen at New York-Idlewild in August 1963. It crashed near Mexico City on December 24, 1966. *(Author)*

almost in the water. Power was applied, but the rear fuselage struck the water and the aircraft settled until the main gear reached the bay floor, with the cabin door sills just above the water. Interestingly, by FAA decree, the precision approach radar (PAR) had been de-commissioned and removed some months previously as few carriers were using it, so no warning of the low approach was transmitted by a ground controller. Many other U.S. domestic airports had suffered a similar loss.

The aircraft was hoisted out of the water onto a huge barge two days later, then taken to the United Air Lines maintenance base at the airport. The cabin was stripped and the entire aircraft flushed out with thousands of gallons of fresh water. All 36 miles of wiring were replaced. In addition, most hydraulic and other systems, including cockpit instrumentation, were overhauled or replaced. The flaps, two pylons plus the left main gear cylinder and bogie were replaced. The engines were in remarkable condition, with only the inlet fan case and gear boxes needing replacement due to corrosion. After four months, on April 26, 1969, the aircraft was back in

the air, at a cost of $4 million. Currently operated by Airborne Express, the DC-8 has accumulated over 60,000 hours to date.

Three major accidents have occurred when ground spoilers or thrust reversers were applied too soon. The first was an Air Canada DC-8-63 landing at Toronto on July 5, 1970. The co-pilot inadvertently selected immediate spoiler deployment instead of merely arming the ground spoilers to activate automatically after touchdown. The aircraft stalled and made a heavy landing, but the pilot elected to attempt a go-around. However, severe damage had been done, including the shedding of one engine and rupture of the wing tanks which caused a fire, leading to an in-flight explosion as the aircraft turned for a new approach.

On September 15, 1970, an Alitalia captain elected to use thrust reverse rather than initiate a go-around, while landing at JFK Airport, New York. The aircraft hit the runway hard, and ground looped, collapsing the gear and breaking the fuselage in half; three engines also separated but, amazingly, there was no fire or deaths, although several injuries resulted.

Cubana DC-8-43 CU-T1201 (ln 127/msn 45611) crashed into the sea shortly after takeoff from Barbados on October 6, 1976. *(H. Oehninger)*

After this excursion from the runway at London-Heathrow in February 1969, DC-8-63CF N8634 (ln 424/msn 46021) was less fortunate six months later during a similar incident at Stockton, California, when it was destroyed by fire. *(Brian Stainer)*

In another landing incident at JFK, on June 23, 1973, the co-pilot of an Icelandic DC-8-61 activated the ground spoilers at an altitude of 25 feet, causing the aircraft to stall and hit the ground tail first, just short of the runway. The left outboard engine was torn off and the main gear collapsed, but everyone survived, and the aircraft was re-built. The National Transportation Safety Board (NTSB) then recommended that the FAA require that "inadvertent operation of any ground deceleration devices be made impossible while in flight." The report was worded this way as the DC-8-62 and -63 were capable of in-flight reverse thrust on the inboard engines, to make steep descents. The Douglas response was that in-flight reverse thrust should only be used when the aircraft was in a clean condition, which would ensure that it was still at altitude, and flying at not less than 190 knots. Douglas added that ground spoilers should only be armed per instructions in the flight manual.

Often overlooked after the initial newsworthy reporting of an accident is the resulting litigation that can go on for several years. A classic example involved a Swissair DC-8-62, HB-IDE, which skidded off the end of a runway at Athens, Greece, on October 8, 1979. Landing at night on a wet run-

way, the pilot touched down normally, applied reverse thrust on schedule, yet still slid off the runway and fell down a 12-foot drop onto a rocky escarpment. Fourteen people were killed, and the Greek authorities promptly charged the pilot with manslaughter and willful negligence. Found guilty, the pilot was sentenced to over five years in jail; Swissair bailed him out and appealed.

The case dragged on until April 28, 1986, when Swissair paid a fine. Disagreement centered on the condition of the runway, which was very greasy from rubber residue and rain. Just prior to the accident, an Olympic 707 had experienced braking problems, and notified the tower. A following DC-10 was warned and deliberately landed short, but the Swissair crew was not informed of this. Thirty minutes after Swissair had crashed, a Finnair DC-8 landed and its captain, used to icy surfaces, notified his airline operations department that it was the slipperiest runway he had ever been exposed to. It was immediately closed down.

Because the traffic flow had just reverted to the normal direction for landing, a large residual area up of rubber build-up had accumulated on the heavy braking area on the runway. The Greeks normally removed this residue by grinding rather

SAS DC-8-62 LN-MOO (ln 270/msn 45822) crashed into the Pacific during a night approach to LAX on January 13, 1969.

(Gerry Markgraf)

Following an accident JAL DC-8-32 JA8003 (ln 93/msn 45420) was rebuilt as a model 53, becoming JA8008. (Author's Collection)

than steam cleaning, which left a polished surface for water to pool on. In addition, the tower personnel had failed to warn the Swissair crew that they were landing downwind, and that windshear was present. The prosecutor's argument was that the pilots should have known that they should land short on a wet runway! Obviously, at the root of this case was insurance liability.

Several incidents of DC-8s losing engines in flight have occurred, but in each case the aircraft has landed safely. In November 1963, as an Eastern DC-8 climbed out of Houston, the pilot reported that they had suddenly lost all airspeed. The aircraft appeared to be in a violent up-draft, so full "nose-down" was applied to the controls. In the ensuing pull-out, the number three engine was torn off. The aircraft made a safe landing at Barksdale AFB, where examination of the flight data recorder confirmed that the aircraft actually incurred a zero airspeed for 4 minutes and 20 seconds! Negative G-forces were also recorded during the push-over. However, subsequent examination of the aircraft showed that a bad leak in the autopilot static line, created by faulty installation below the cockpit floor, may have caused misleading instrument readings.

Another incident took place during a JAL training flight in December 1963. While simulating rudder hydraulic failure with two engines out, airspeed fell below 120 knots. The pilot pushed the nose down, brought both left engines, which had been idling, to full power but failed to re-trim the rudder. The DC-8 stalled and entered a right-hand spin at 12,500 feet. After five turns, recovery was made, but both outboard engines had been torn off. A safe landing was made at Okinawa.

To date, no DC-8 has ever been lost due to in-flight structural failure, though this situation could have happened in the mid-1970s. Early in 1977, incidents of skin cracking around the pylon areas of a few model 62s and 63s were discovered. Inspections led to the discovery of some skin cracks on a Braniff model -62 and a CP Air -63. Both aircraft had reached 35,000 hours, so the problem was initially thought to be time-related. Douglas proposed a comparatively cheap repair scheme which would add another 15,000 hours of airframe life, and asked that all aircraft reaching 35,000 hours be x-rayed and tested by ultrasound techniques. Braniff found three other cases, all in the number two pylon attachment area.

However, during re-work of the damaged aircraft, it was discovered that the spar cap itself was cracking around skin fastener holes, a much more serious situation. The aircraft structure was strong enough to survive with either the skin or spar cap cracking, but not both at the same time. The previous repair scheme was abandoned, and a much more stringent requirement for earlier mandatory inspection was issued for the entire model 62/63 fleet. An Airworthiness Directive which followed required an extensive, $200,000 modification, plus substantial down-time. It called for replacement of

A Close Call

An Alitalia DC-8-43, I-DIWM, survived a hit by an air-to-air missile on June 26, 1970 while flying about 40 miles east of Damascus, Syria, in the area of air battle between Israeli Mirages and Syrian MiGs. The DC-8 was en route from Tehran to Rome under control of the Damascus tower at the time, and its crew had been advised to leave Syrian air space and proceed to Beirut because of the danger. Cruising at 29,500 feet, a severe jolt was felt, followed by an altitude loss of 3,000 feet before the crew stabilized the aircraft. The pilot initially believed that he had struck a light aircraft. The missile penetrated the left wing just behind the front spar, between the engine pods. It entered from above and passed through the wing without exploding. In addition to the 2-foot diameter hole, considerable shrapnel damage was done to the flap hydraulic system, left tailplane and the engine pods. The left outboard engine and its fuel supply were shut down and, with Damascus airport temporarily closed, the aircraft was diverted to Beirut where the crew made a normal landing after lowering the flaps using the emergency system. Needless to say, the warring factions blamed each other for this near-disaster.

The DC-8 was repaired and re-entered service a few months later. Sold by Alitalia in 1975, it was operated by Sterling Philippines until retired in 1983, with only 35,000 hours on its airframe. Strangely, the mysterious loss of a DC-9-15 belonging to Italian domestic airline Itavia, on June 27, 1980, over the Tyrrhenian Sea, was also attributed to a stray air-to-air missile of unknown origin.

the front lower spar cap, renewal of a section of the lower wing skin and new structural components in the area surrounding the four pylons.

The Douglas facility at Tulsa set up a production line to handle the modifications, but most airlines elected to carry out their own repair work.

In May 1988, Douglas announced that it had sold the rights to manufacture spare parts for all Douglas products from the DC-3 to the DC-8, plus the DC-10, to Gulfstream Aerospace. This allowed Gulfstream, at its Oklahoma City factory, to purchase raw materials and fabricate any part or tooling required from technical data supplied by Douglas. Over 200 people were hired to handle the new program.

Following the Aloha 737 incident in 1989, in which the forward cabin roof peeled off, the U.S. Government set up a task force to examine aging aircraft. The DC-8 fell into this category, and after a review of all the applicable service bulletins, only minimal changes were required as the DC-8s had suffered very few problems from corrosion compared to other manufacturers. Most of the changes recommended were to replace certain fittings as specific flight times were reached, as a precautionary measure.

In an effort to reduce the chance of mid-air collisions, Bendix/King developed a Threat Alert/Collision Avoidance System (TCAS) in the mid 1980s. A six-month trial using a United Airlines DC-8 and 737 ended in November 1988, during which the system was used for over 2,000 hours on 1,224 sectors. Traffic advisories were experienced on the average every 2.2 hours or every 1.3 sectors. Resolution advisories, where the system advised the pilots to take action due to conflicting traffic, averaged one every 28 flight hours and one every 17 sectors. Today, TCAS has become standard on all jet transports in the United States. With the newly proposed "Free Flights" in the United States, which essentially abolishes air-lanes, it will become a more important development.

Unusual Incidents

While en route to Johannesburg in late 1961, a steward, working in the first-class galley of a Scandinavian DC-8 felt a sharp ankle pain. On looking down, he discovered a snake, which had presumably boarded at the previous stop in Nairobi. Other crew members killed the snake and administered first-aid. He received full medical treatment on landing and suffered no lasting effects. SAS claimed the dubious record of the highest known instance of snakebite – at 35,000 feet!

A less amusing event took place on January 21, 1980, when United Air Lines received a series of phone calls demanding a $1 million ransom. The caller claimed to have placed a bomb aboard a DC-8 that was en route from Los Angeles to Hawaii. He indicated that the bomb had armed itself upon reaching 5,000 feet, and was set to explode when the aircraft descended below that level. After a stewardess located a crude container in an aft lavatory and alerted the crew, a decision was made to return to the mainland and land at Colorado Springs Airport, which is just over 6,000 feet above sea-level. Military bomb disposal experts removed the device from the DC-8 and, after careful examination, announced that it was a very complex fake. The FBI became involved and many rumors circulated of complicated pay-off schemes to the extortionist, but no one was ever arrested or charged in the incident. Shortly afterwards, a spate of similar threats were received by several airlines, but none proved to be legitimate.

A more tragic event took place in Australia in February 1970, when a stow-away fell from a wheel well of a Japan Air Lines DC-8-62 as it took off from Sydney, en route to Tokyo. The 14-year old boy, who had a history of running away, had climbed into the opening and sat on the closed landing gear door. Unfortunately for him, when the door opened to allow the wheels to retract, he fell out at a height of about 150 feet.

Though it has been bettered many times since, a 1961 record around-the-world trip was made by six young ladies from Iran, Pakistan, Thailand Sweden, the Philippines and Japan in 50 hours, 15 minutes. Their journey started in Tokyo, flew via the polar route to Europe, then on to Tokyo via Asia, all on SAS DC-8 services.

Chapter X
DC-8s That Might Have Been

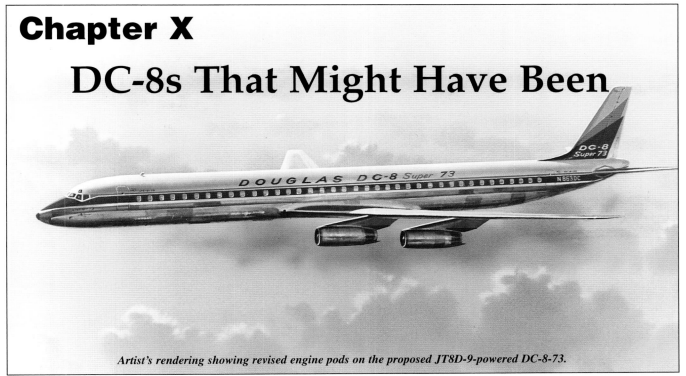

Artist's rendering showing revised engine pods on the proposed JT8D-9-powered DC-8-73.

Probably one of the first DC-8 development studies to be launched started in 1958 with an attempt to develop a medium-sized jetliner compatible with the type, for short- to medium-stage lengths. By mid-1959, brochures being shown to the airlines described a scaled-down DC-8 "look-alike," powered by four Pratt & Whitney JT10D fan engines of 8,250 pounds thrust each. Designated as the DC-9, it carried a maximum of 92 passengers, five-abreast in DC-8-type Palomar seats. It had a wingspan of 94 feet, overall length of 103 feet and a MTOW of 120,000 pounds. Eventually, it was re-configured to a twin-engined layout and, after several reiterations, developed into the DC-9 of today.

Shortly before the DC-8-60 Series was launched in 1965, the advanced design team at Long Beach had already begun looking into further developments of the type, mostly in response to specific customer requirements. Many different combinations of fuselage lengths, engine operating weights and range requirements were studied. The following are samples of some of the more interesting variations. From them, it is easy to see how the DC-8-70 Series of today was created by essentially the same people responsible for the development of the production DC-8s.

First in the series was a growth version of the DC-8-61, in late-1964. Identified as the DC-8-71, changes included raising the MTOW from 325,000 to 360,000 pounds, and adding tapered leading-edge "glove" tanks at the wing roots, which increased the total fuel capacity by 1,200 gallons. The tank had actually been designed earlier and flight-tested on the "Ducted Fan" DC-8, N109RD, during the long-duct flight trials. Some structural changes were required, including frame stiffening, heavier skin panels and a strengthened landing gear. The fuselage was shortened by 40 inches, or one frame. The engines specified were Pratt & Whitney JT3D-5A turbofans of 21,000 pounds static thrust, encased in long-duct pods.

In 1965, attention turned to improving the DC-8-62, by increasing the MTOW by 5,000 pounds. Part of the concept, designated DC-8-64, included adding the previously mentioned leading edge "glove" tank, but this created a problem in that the tank leading edge at the fuselage side intersection interfered with the forward baggage door and the pitot static ports. To overcome this, a 40-inch plug was inserted so that the door moved further forward, also allowing a maximum seating capacity increase to 204. This resulted in the need to enlarge the over-wing emergency exits as the aircraft was exit-limited to 189 by FAA standards. Apart from some strengthening of wing skins, landing gear and an additional fuselage frame, no other changes were required. The engines were unchanged from the JT3D-3B.

There was a slight loss in range with a full payload, and the project was eventually dropped. Another option looked at was to stretch the aircraft and increase the MTOW, but not

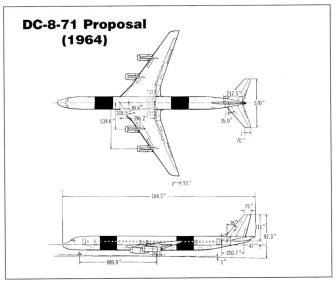

DC-8-71 Proposal (1964)

119

Model 83

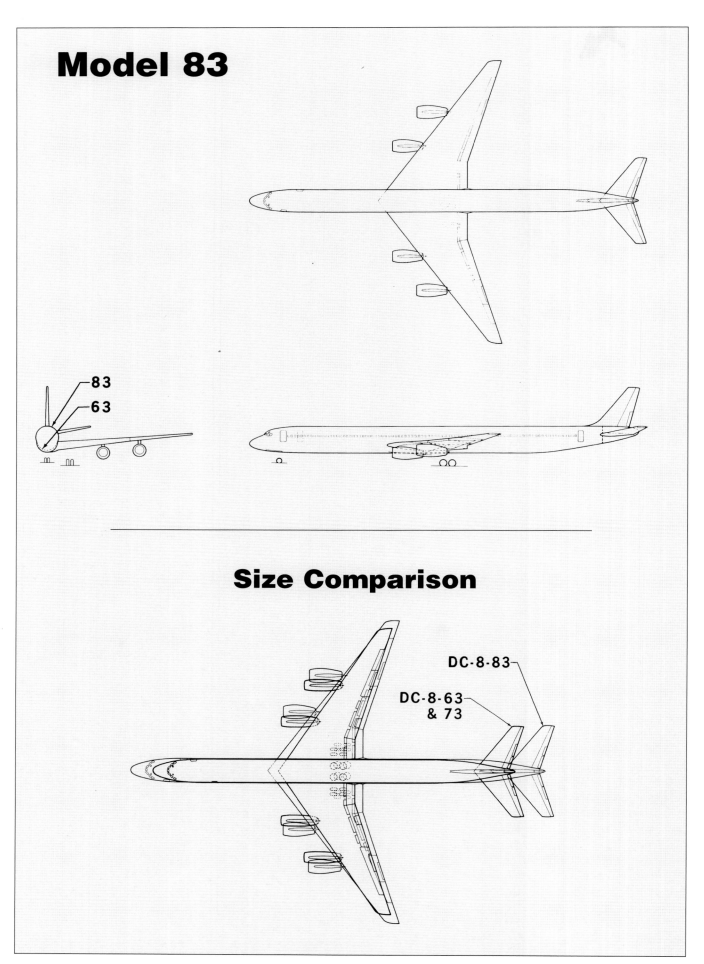

83
63

Size Comparison

DC-8-83
DC-8-63 & 73

add the tanks. Eventually, the -62 came off the line with the higher thrust JT3D-7 engines (19,000-pound thrust), which allowed the MTOW to increase to 350,000 pounds.

In 1966, in response to the Boeing 727-200, Douglas investigated re-engining the DC-8-50 with Pratt & Whitney JT8D-5 engines developing 12,000 pounds thrust. This was the same engine fitted to the DC-9 and the 737. The model number applied to the study was DC-8-70. Two different approaches were made, one using the standard Series 50 pylon and the other incorporating the long-duct pod with cutback pylons on the Series 50 wing. Designed for a 2,000-mile range with 189 passengers, the aircraft was much lighter than the Series 50. It was targeted at existing DC-8 operators and traded the extra engine thrust for airframe and cockpit standardization. Initial and operating costs were undoubtedly the primary reasons that this version was never built.

A similar approach to the DC-8-70 was the DC-8-73, a light weight model 63 designed to meet British European Airways (BEA) requirement for an "airbus" with a maximum range of 2,000 miles. Again, the JT3Bs were replaced by four 14,000-pound thrust Pratt & Whitney JT8D-7 engines, in the long-duct pods. The airframe was lightened and fuel tankage reduced to 75,000 pounds.

To confuse the issue, another version of the DC-8-73, studied in 1965, was intended to extend the range of the model 63. Fitted with Pratt & Whitney JT8D-15 engines (15,500 pounds thrust), it also had additional tankage via a larger leading edge "glove" tank. Other areas considered for additional fuel capacity included belly tanks, and fitting tanks in the horizontal stabilizer and fin. The version was considerably heavier, although its external dimensions remained the same. Primarily aimed at BOAC, it was designed to operate nonstop with a full payload on the London-Los Angeles route. As a marketing gimmick, the presentation to BOAC identified the aircraft as the DC-10! BOAC eventually decided that a larger aircraft was needed and opted for the Boeing 747. Later versions of the -63 were fitted with 19,000-pound thrust JT3D-7s, which allowed the MTOW to increase to 355,000 pounds. With some minor structural and landing gear changes, maximum landing weight was also increased to 258,000 pounds.

Yet another version of the DC-8-73 appeared in 1967, again based on the DC-8-61 and powered by Pratt & Whitney JT8D-9s of 14,500-pounds thrust. With a ramp weight of around 300,000 pounds, it was a light-weight version, with a range of around 2,000 miles.

Another nuance considered was to add triple-slotted flaps to the Series 63 to improve take-off performance, particularly on hot days. It reduced the field length requirements by 800 feet, and also slowed approach speeds by 10 knots, with a slight range penalty for the increased drag from the new flap linkage.

At the request of an African copper mining company, a small project team investigated building a "DC-8-60 Junior" in the mid-1960s. The idea was to ferry copper ingots in 100,000-pound shipments to Europe. Due to the high density of copper, very little volume was required, so only a short fuselage would have been required. At the time, the DC-8-63F was the only jet transport capable of lifting 100,000-pound payloads over the required distance. The project was dropped because this market was too limited to absorb associated development costs.

In late 1965, the ultimate stretch concept emerged as the DC-8-83. A radical departure in many ways, the wing span was increased by ten feet to 158 feet, 4 inches, with the insert added at the wing root to obtain maximum volume for increased fuel capacity and heavier landing gear stowage. It also maintained the wing stiffness. The overall length was stretched another 25 feet, to 212 feet, 4 inches, via two plugs. To stiffen the fuselage structure, the lower fuselage was increased in radius, while the upper radius remaining unchanged. Seating capacity increased to 302 passengers at 34-inch pitch, requiring an additional pair of passenger boarding doors forward of the wing.

The power plants, identified only as "C-5 Commercial" in studies, were high-bypass engines of around 28,000-pounds thrust, de-rated from the 40,000-pound thrust examples being offered by both General Electric and Pratt & Whitney for the C-5A military transport competition which was running at the same time. It was designed to carry an 80,000-pound payload from London to Los Angeles, which equated to a full passenger complement and 28,000 pounds of cargo. Belly capacity was over 4,000 cubic feet compared to the model 63's capacity of 2,525 cubic feet.

The final version of DC-8 development was to widen the upper fuselage lobe, in an attempt to bring the level of comfort to that equal to an eight-abreast 747 seating layout. This project, designated DC-8-74, appeared in 1967 and was based on the previously mentioned JT8D-9 powered -73 proposal. The upper fuselage cross-section was increased from 147 to 164 inches at the widest point. The intention was to add more space at the shoulder height of a seated passenger. At the floor level, the cabin width remained unchanged. This would have been achieved by splitting the fuselage on the centerline and adding an insert. However, it was believed that considerable strengthening would have been required as departure from a true radius would create pressurization problems.

The seating, in a 34-inch seat pitch configuration, would have been reduced from the 242 of the model 61 to only 218, using the proposed new larger seats. The additional structural weight was partially offset by the reduced passenger load, but in general, the operating weights of the model 83 exceeded those of the -73 by 2,000 to 3,000 pounds and, with the larger cross-section adding increased drag, performance would suffer. Naturally, the seat/mile economics fared poorly against the model 61 and it could not have operated the critical New York-West Coast nonstop routes with more than 213 passengers and their luggage.

This version was also considered as a freighter; its larger cross section would increase the cargo volume from 8,140 cubic feet to 10,150 cubic feet in the upper lobe. The standard cargo door measuring 85 inches high by 140 inches wide would have been increased in width to 252 inches, to facilitate loading of oversize cargo. The project was eventually dropped when work was initiated on the proposal for a 200-seat wide-body twin-jet study requested by American Airlines. The new project, known as the D-966, eventually evolved into a tri-jet called the DC-10.

Unusual Color Schemes

African Safari DC-8-33 5Y-ASA (ln 75/msn 45379) was eventually replaced by a more conservatively painted DC-8-63. (ALPS)

To celebrate the United States Bicentennial in 1976, Overseas National Airways developed two unique liveries, applied to DC-8-32 N1776R (ln 60/msn 45602) and DC-8-21 N1976P (ln 149/msn 45435). (H. Oehninger & Harry Sievers)

EC-CAM (ln 56/msn 45427), a DC-8-21 of Air Spain, formerly N8606 with Eastern. (Author)

SpearAir, a Finnish charter company, operated DC-8-33 OH-SOB (ln 60/msn 45602) for two years on inclusive tour flights. The aircraft later passed to ONA (see photo Page 122). *(see photo Page 122)* *(John Wegg)*

Probably the most photographed DC-8, Braniff's model 62 N1805 (ln 304/msn 45899) "Flying Colors" designed by Alexander Calder, seen at Miami. It is now with Rich International. *(Author's Collection)*

Epilogue

As recently as 1991, several American operators discussed with Douglas yet another approach to extending the life of the remaining DC-8-60s. Led by Al Weisman, then president of Airborne Express, the carriers suggested that the existing four JT3B power plants could be replaced by two de-rated Pratt & Whitney 2000 series engines, located at the in-board engine positions, and fairing over the outboard pylon locations on the wing. Though no design studies were ever completed by Douglas, it was evident that modification of the wing structure would be far more complex than originally envisioned. The estimated cost was at least $15 million per aircraft. The idea was subsequently abandoned because many DC-10s and TriStars were becoming available, at reasonable prices, for conversion to freighters.

At the same time, a survey was undertaken to establish whether it would be worth re-opening a production line to convert the remaining Series 60s into Series 70s using the CFM-56 engines, but insufficient aircraft remained to make it a viable proposition.

Whether the DC-8 will soldier on for as many years as its famous forebear, the DC-3, remains to be seen. To put things into perspective, it is worth remembering that high-time DC-3s have been re-built many times over, something that has never really been contemplated for jetliners of any kind. In addition, the DC-3's average annual utilization was nowhere near the 3,500 hours per year flown in the heyday of the DC-8. Today, with overnight package flying making up the bulk of DC-8 operations, the average annual utilization and number of cycles has dropped to around half that amount.

At the time of writing, monthly flight/cycle data for over 235 DC-8s is still reported to Douglas, with approximately 75 more aircraft listed as "in storage;" some will undoubtedly return to active duty. Many have accumulated less than 70,000 hours. The high-time aircraft, N836UP, a DC-8-73CF of UPS, has already exceeded 88,000 hours in only 24,000 cycles. The lowest time aircraft still active is a DC-8-54F, N7064H, currently operated by Fine Air. Originally delivered to United in October 1968, the aircraft has flown only 37,000 hours during 16,000 cycles. So, it is not unreasonable to anticipate that many of the remaining examples will last another 10 years to 15 years at least.

As mentioned earlier, the water-tank tests indicated that the DC-8 could safely fly at least 140,000 cycles. Currently, a UPS DC-8-71F, N709UP, has the highest recorded number, less than 48,000 cycles in about 72,000 hours. A Trans Continental Airlines DC-8-62, N803MG, holds the record for the least number of cycles, with just over 13,000 in 45,000 hours of flying. Certainly the remaining structural life of most of the aircraft still in service will allow them to operate well into the 21st century. The real threat to their future is likely to come when the proposed FAR 36, Stage 4 noise restrictions come into effect, at a still undetermined date, though operators of the Series 70s may still find an economical way to meet even those standards.

The DC-8 fleet statistics are impressive; over 30 million flight hours have accumulated in just over 11.5 million cycles. To date, the number of airlines that have owned or leased DC-8s has reached 350 and they may yet serve with many more, a far cry from the original 48 operators that took delivery from the Long Beach factory. Regardless of what the future may hold, the DC-8 has already amply demonstrated that it carried on the great Douglas traditions of design flexibility and structural integrity.

Appendix I

WRITE-OFFS

(LISTED BY DATE)

Airline	Type	Registration MSN/Line No.	Date	Comments
United	DC-8-12	N8013U 45290/022	12-16-60	Mid-air collision with TWA 1049 Constellation over Brooklyn, New York.
Aeronaves de Mexico	DC-8-21	XA-XAX 45432/105	01-19-61	Aborted takeoff at New York-Idlewild Check pilot retarded power.
KLM	DC-8-53	PH-DCL 45615/131	05-30-61	Crashed off Portuguese coast, en route Lisbon– Santa Maria, Azores. Operating VIASA flight.
United	DC-8-12	N8040U 45307/146	07-11-61	Crashed while landing at Denver, Colorado. Thrust reverser malfunction on port engines.
Alitalia	DC-8-43	I-DIWD 45631/160	07-07-62	Crashed into high ground during approach to Bombay, India at night.
Panair do Brazil	DC-8-33	PP-PDT 45273/121	08-20-62	Incorrect stabilizer trim; failed to rotate on takeoff at Rio de Janiero. Crashed into sea.
Trans-Canada	DC-8-54JT	CF-TJN 45654/179	11-29-63	Crashed shortly after takeoff from Montreal. Horizontal stabilizer trim problem.
Eastern	DC-8-21	N8607 45428/061	02-25-64	Crashed in Lake Pontchartrain after take-off from New Orleans. Pitch trim problem.
Trans Caribbean	DC-8-54JT	N8784R 45769/215	10-24-65	Destroyed by fire at Miami.
Canadian Pacific	DC-8-43	CF-CPK 45761/237	03-04-66	Undershot runway at Tokyo-Haneda. Hit sea wall.
Air New Zealand	DC-8-52	ZK-NZB 45751/231	07-04-66	Crashed on takeoff at Auckland, New Zealand. Crew training flight.
Aeronaves de Mexico	DC-8-51	XA-PEI 45652/176	08-13-66	Crashed on training flight near Acapulco, Mexico.
Aeronaves de Mexico	DC-8-51	XA-NUS 45633/162	12-24-66	Crash-landed on dry lake near Mexico City, Mexico.
VARIG	DC-8-33	PP-PEA 45253/005	03-04-67	Crashed on approach to Robertsfield, Monrovia, Liberia.
Delta	DC-8-51	N802E 45409/019	03-30-67	Crashed on approach to New Orleans. Crew training flight.

Airline	Type	Registration MSN/Line No.	Date	Comments
Air Canada	DC-8-54JT	CF-TJM 45653/178	05-19-67	Crashed on approach to Uplands Airport, Ottawa. Crew training flight.
Capitol	DC-8-31	N4903C 45277/094	04-28-68	Crashed at Atlantic City, New Jersey. Crew training flight.
KLM	DC-8-53	PH-DCH 45383/120	06-29-68	Destroyed in hangar fire at Amsterdam-Schiphol.
Alitalia	DC-8-43	I-DIWF 45630/159	08-02-68	Crashed on approach to Milan-Malpensa.
SAS	DC-8-62	LN-MOO 45822/270	01-13-69	Undershot at Los Angeles and crashed into the Pacific Ocean at night.
Seaboard World	DC-8-63CF	N8634 46021/424	10-16-69	Ran off runway during rejected takeoff at Stockton, California.
SAS	DC-8-62	SE-DBE 45823/279	04-19-70	Caught fire while taxiing at Rome-Fiumicino.
Air Canada	DC-8-63	CF-TIW 46114/526	07-05-70	Crashed on go-around after aborted heavy landing at Toronto, Canada.
Flying Tigers	DC-8-63AF	N785FT 46005/412	07-27-70	Undershot on approach to Okinawa. Hit reef.
Trans International	DC-8-63CF	N4863T 45951/414	09-08-70	Stalled on takeoff from New York-JFK. Elevators jammed.
Swissair	DC-8-53	HB-IDD 45656/191	09-13-70	Blown up by terrorists at Dawson Field, Jordan after being hijacked.
Alitalia	DC-8-62	I-DIWZ 46026/452	09-15-70	Hard landing at New York-JFK.
Capitol	DC-8-63CF	N4904C 46060/472	11-27-70	Destroyed after aborted takeoff at Anchorage, Alaska.
Alitalia	DC-8-43	I-DIWB 45625/144	05-05-72	Crashed into Mt. Lunga on approach to Palermo, Sicily. Strayed from correct flight path.
Japan Air Lines	DC-8-53	JA8012 45680/213	06-14-72	Crashed on approach to New Delhi, India. Attempted VFR landing in IFR conditions.
Iberia	DC-8-52	EC-ARA 45617/136	07-06-72	Crashed in sea near Las Palmas, Canary Islands.
Japan Air Lines	DC-8-53	JA8013 45681/214	09-23-72	Ran off runway at Bombay, India
Japan Air Lines	DC-8-62	JA8040 46057/474	11-28-72	Crashed on takeoff at Moscow. Icing caused engine damage, aircraft stalled.
Air Canada	DC-8-53	CF-TIJ 45962/402	06-21-73	Caught fire on ground at Toronto.

Airline	Type	Registration MSN/Line No.	Date	Comments
World Airways	DC-8-63CF	N802WA 46146/536	09-08-73	Crashed into Mt. Dutton, Cold Bay, Alaska.
Thai International	DC-8-33	HS-TGU 45526/089	05-10-73	Overshot while landing at Katmandu, Nepal.
Airlift International	DC-8-63CF	N6164A 46144/532	03-23-74	Destroyed by fire at Travis AFB, California
Garuda Indonesian	DC-8-55JT	PH-MBH 45818/242	12-04-74	Crashed into Laxabana Hill, Sri Lanka.
Cubana	DC-8-43	CU-T1200 45638/156	03-18-76	Mid-air collision with Cubana An-24 near Havana. DC-8 lost part of outer wing, but landed safely.
Cubana	DC-8-43	CU-T1201 45611/127	10-06-76	Crashed into sea near Barbados. Bomb exploded shortly after takeoff.
Japan Air Lines	DC-8-62AF	JA8054 46148/553	01-13-77	Crashed after takeoff from Anchorage, Alaska. Carrying cattle.
Overseas National	DC-8-63CF	N8635 46050/430	03-04-77	Undershot runway, crashed at Niamey, Niger.
Philippine Air	DC-8-53	RP-C803 45937/324	04-19-77	Skidded off runway at Tokyo-Haneda during takeoff.
Japan Air Lines	DC-8-62	JA8051 46152/550	09-27-77	Crashed on approach to Kuala Lumpur, Malaysia during thunderstorm.
Charlotte Aircraft.	DC-8-33	N8170A 45270/112	12-11-77	Caught fire while refuelling at Lake City, Fla.
United	DC-8-54JT	N8047U 45880/275	12-18-77	Crashed into Ed's Peak, Wasatch Mountains, near Salt Lake City, Utah.
Iberia	DC-8-63	EC-BMX 45930/378	03-03-78	Over-ran runway during landing at Santiago, Spain. Broke in two.
Loftleidir	DC-8-63CF	TF-FLA 46020/415	11-15-78	Hit trees during over-shoot at Colombo, Sri Lanka.
United	DC-8-61	N8082U 45972/357	12-28-78	Crashed near Portland, Oregon. Fuel exhaustion.
Swissair	DC-8-62	HB-IDE 45919/312	10-08-79	Overran on wet runway at Athens, Greece.
Aero Peru	DC-8-43F	OB-R1143 45598/057	08-01-80	Crashed near Mexico City.
Aero Peru	DC-8-33F	N715UA 45386/062	09-11-80	Crashed near Iquitos, Peru.
Overseas National	DC-8-61	N913R 46128/514	01-15-81	Destroyed in hangar fire at Luxembourg.

Airline	Type	Registration MSN/Line No.	Date	Comments
Japan Air Lines	DC-8-61	JA8061 45889/291	02-09-82	Undershot landing at Tokyo-Haneda Crashed in Tokyo Bay.
United	DC-8-54JT	N8053U 46010/406	01-11-83	Stalled after liftoff at Detroit-Metro. Improper stabilizer trim setting.
UTA	DC-8-63PF	F-BOLL 46096/499	03-10-84	Destroyed by terrorist bomb, N'djamena, Chad.
Aeroservicios Ecuatorias	DC-8-55JT	HC-BKN 45754/225	09-18-84	Crashed after takeoff from Quito, Ecuador
LAC Colombia	DC-8-53	HK2380 45879/268	09-18-84	Damaged beyond repair after over-run at Barranquilla, Colombia.
Arrow Air	DC-8-63PF	N950JW 46058/433	12-12-85	Crashed on takeoff at Gander, Newfoundland. Not de-iced prior to departure.
Arax Airlines	DC-8-55CF	5N-ARH 45859/253	03-31-88	Crashed on takeoff at Cairo, Egypt. Carrying cattle.
Gabon Government	DC-8-73CF	TR-LTZ 46053/446	04-13-88	Attempted to take off from taxiway at Frankfurt. Over ran into soft ground. Remains stored unrepaired.
Surinam Airways	DC-8-62	N1809E 46107/498	06-07-89	Undershot runway and hit trees at Surinam. Pilot not DC-8 qualified.
ATI	DC-8-62F	N730PL 46141/552	3-12-91	Destroyed by fire after aborted takeoff at New York-JFK.
Nationair	DC-8-61	C-GMXQ 45982/345	07-11-91	Hydraulic failure after tires burst on takeoff at Jeddah, Saudi Arabia, causing wheelwell fire.
Burlington Air Express	DC-8-63	N794AL 45923/383	02-15-92	Crashed on approach to Toledo, Ohio, in fog.
MK Air Cargo	DC-8-54JT	9G-MKB 45860/256	02-15-92	Crashed on approach to Kano, Nigeria.
American Int'l..	DC-8-61	N25UA 46127/510	08-18-93	Crashed short of runway at U.S. Naval Air Station, Guantanamo Bay, Cuba.
Fine Air	DC-8-51F	HK3816X 45685/204	05-21-94	Nose gear collapsed on takeoff roll at Medellin, Colombia. Damaged beyond repair.
ATI	DC-8-63	N782AL 45929/367	02-16-95	Crashed on 3-engine takeoff at Kansas City (International), Mo. Lost directional stability.
Millon Air	DC-8-54JT	N43UA 45677/199	04-28-95	Crashed short of runway at Guatemala City, Guatemala.
Affretair	DC-8-55F	Z-WSB 45805/244	01-28-96	Over ran runway at Harare, Zimbabwe. Nose broken off. Hydraulic failure suspected.
LAC Colombia	DC-8-55F	HK3979X 45882/282	02-04-96	Crashed after takeoff from Asuncion, Paraguay. Engine fire.

Appendix II
TEST REGISTRATIONS

Ship	MSN	Registr.	Model	Delivered	Customer
002	45278	N8018D	21 (DM)	N8001U	United
003	45279	N8028D	12 (DM)	N8002U	United
004	45280	N8038D	11 (DM)	N8003U	United
007	45255	N8068D	33 (OW)	N802PA	Pan Am
009	45442	N6577C	41 (OW)	CF-TJA	Trans-Canada
018	45443	N6578C	41 (OW)	CF-TJB	Trans-Canada
071	45567	N9601Z	32 (OW)	F-BJLA	UAT
120	45383	N9603Z	53 (OW)	PH-DCH	KLM
126	45614	N9605Z	53 (OW)	PH-DCK	KLM
130	45623	N9604Z	43 (OW)	CF-CPA	Canadian Pacific
154	45607	N9607Z	53 (OW)	PI-C801	Philippine
155	45608	N9608Z	53 (OW)	PH-DCP	KLM
175	45640	N9609Z	54JT	CF-TJL	Trans-Canada
178	45653	N9612Z	54JT	CF-TJM	Trans-Canada
217	45750	N9683Z	52 (OW)	ZK-NZA	Air New Zealand
265	45765	N2310B	55L	PK-GJD	Garuda
270	45822	N1501U	62	LN-MOO	SAS
279	45823	N1502U	62	SE-DBE	SAS
286	45903	N1503U	63	PH-DEA	KLM
293	45901	N1504U	63	PH-DEB	KLM
307	45909	N1505U	62	I-DIWN	Alitalia
327	45927	N19B	63	CF-CPP	CP Air
361	45961	N8964U	62CF	I-DIWQ	Alitalia
367	45929	N19B	63	CF-CPS	CP Air
542	46130	N8731U	62CF	OH-LFY	Finnair

Note: DAC also used N19B on numerous DC-9s and DC-10s.

Ship One on an early test flight. A frangible crew escape hatch is visible under the forward fuselage.

Appendix III

Dimensions

MODEL NUMBER	-11	-21	-31	-41	53	61	62	63
AREAS (SQ. FT.):								
WING — TOTAL	2,758.2	2,772.8	2,772.8	2,772.8	2,883.6	2,883.6	2,926.8	2,926.8
FLAP — TOTAL	456.9	456.9	456.9	456.9	456.9	456.9	456.9	456.9
AILERON — TOTAL	161.6	161.6	161.6	161.6	161.6	161.6	161.6	161.6
HORIZONTAL TAIL	559.1	559.1	559.1	559.1	559.1	559.1	559.1	559.1
STABILIZER	391.2	391.2	391.2	391.2	391.2	391.2	391.2	391.2
ELEVATOR	167.9	167.9	167.9	167.9	167.9	167.9	167.9	167.9
VERTICAL TAIL	351.7	351.7	351.7	351.7	351.7	351.7	351.7	351.7
FIN	222.9	222.9	222.9	222.9	222.9	222.9	222.9	222.9
RUDDER	128.8	128.8	128.8	128.8	128.8	128.8	128.8	128.8
WING:								
SPAN (FT)	139.70	142.36	142.36	142.36	142.36	142.36	148.36	148.36
ROOT CHORD (IN.)	380.80	380.80	380.80	380.80	396.20	396.20	396.20	396.20
TIP CHORD (IN.)	93.00	87.50	87.50	87.50	91.00	91.00	78.16	78.16
MAC (IN.)	266.00	263.20	263.20	263.20	275.90	275.90	227.75	272.75
ASPECT RATIO	7.10	7.30	7.30	7.30	7.00	7.00	7.52	7.52
TAPER RATIO	0.244	0.230	0.230	0.230	0.230	0.230	0.197	0.197
DIHEDRAL (DEG)	6.50	6.50	6.50	6.50	6.50	6.50	6.50	6.50
SWEEPBACK (DEG)	30.60	30.00	30.60	30.60	30.60	30.60	30.60	30.60
HORIZONTAL TAIL:								
SPAN (IN.)	570.00	570.00	570.00	570.00	570.00	570.00	570.00	570.00
ROOT CHORD (IN.)	212.50	212.50	212.50	212.50	212.50	212.50	212.50	212.50
TIP CHORD (IN.)	70.00	70.00	70.00	70.00	70.00	70.00	70.00	70.00
ASPECT RATIO	4.00	4.00	4.00	4.00	4.00	4.00	4.00	4.00
TAPER RATIO	0.329	0.329	0.329	0.329	0.329	0.329	0.329	0.329
DIHEDRAL (DEG)	10.00	10.00	10.00	10.00	10.00	10.00	10.00	10.00
SWEEPBACK (DEG)	35.00	35.00	35.00	35.00	35.00	35.00	35.00	35.00
VERTICAL TAIL:								
SPAN (IN.)	311.00	311.00	311.00	311.00	311.00	311.00	311.00	311.00
ROOT CHORD (IN.)	250.70	250.70	250.70	250.70	250.70	250.70	250.70	250.70
TIP CHORD (IN.)	75.00	75.00	75.00	75.00	75.00	75.00	75.00	75.00
ASPECT RATIO	1.90	1.90	1.90	1.90	1.90	1.90	1.90	1.90
TAPER RATIO	0.299	0.299	0.299	0.299	0.299	0.299	0.299	0.299
SWEEPBACK (DEG)	35.00	35.00	35.00	35.00	35.00	35.00	35.00	35.00
ALIGHTING GEAR:								
MAIN WHEEL SIZE	17.00-18	17.00-18	17.00-18	17.00-18	17.00-18	17.00-18	17.00-18	17.00-18
NOSE WHEEL SIZE	11.00-14	11.00-14	11.00-14	11.00-14	11.00-14	11.00-14	11.00-14	11.00-14
MAIN TIRE SIZE	44 x 16	44 x 16	44 x 16	44 x 16	44 x 16	44 x 16	44 x 16	44.5 x 16.5
NOSE TIRE SIZE	34 x 11	34 x 11	34 x 11	34 x 11	34 x 11	34 x 11	34 x 11	34 x 11
MAIN GEAR TREAD (IN.)	250.00	250.00	250.00	250.00	250.00	250.00	250.00	250.00
WHEEL BASE (IN.)	689.90	689.90	689.90	689.90	689.90	929.90	729.90	929.90
FUSELAGE:								
HEIGHT, EXTERNAL (IN.)	162.50	162.50	162.50	162.50	162.50	162.50	162.50	162.50
WIDTH, EXTERNAL (IN.)	147.00	147.00	147.00	147.00	147.00	147.00	147.00	147.00
LENGTH (FT)	146.30	146.30	146.30	146.30	146.30	183.00	153.00	183.00
OVERALL CLEARANCE:								
HEIGHT (FT)	42.30	42.30	42.30	42.30	42.30	42.30	42.30	42.40
LENGTH (FT)	150.70	150.70	150.70	150.70	150.70	187.40	157.40	187.40
WIDTH (FT)	142.36	142.36	142.36	142.36	142.36	142.36	148.36	148.36

This rare shot of Ship One in National Airlines colors was received shortly before the publication deadline. National was first to operate N8008D, between June 1961 and May 1962.   *(James W. Hawkins photo via Mario Mattarelli)*

Appendix IV

DC-8 SPECIFICATIONS AT FIRST FLIGHT

		Domestic 1st Class	Domestic 1st Class	Intercon Mixed Cl.	Intercon Mixed Cl.	Intercon Mixed Cl.
Engines		JT3C-6	JT4A-3	JT4A-3	JT4A-9	RCo-12
Max. takeoff wt.	(lb)	265,000	265,000	287,500	310,000	310,000
Max. landing weight	(lb)	189,000	189,000	194,000	199,500	199,500
Zero fuel weight	(lb)	161,200	164,550	170,550	176,500	174,600
Operating empty weight	(lb)	122,698	124,977	130,092	132,310	130,164
Space limited payload	(lb)	33,040	33,040	35,680	35,680	35,680
Passengers		116	116	132	132	132
Cargo	(lb)	13,900	13,900	13,900	13,900	13,900
Cargo volume	(cu.ft)	1,390	1,390	1,390	1,390	1,390
Range	(Statute Miles)	3,900	4,100	4,500	5,030	5,200

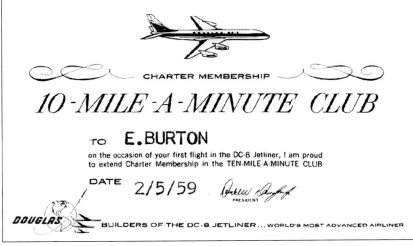

These souvenirs of the early DC-8 days were handed out by Douglas Public Relations. Both bear the name of the airplane's chief designer, Ed Burton. (Courtesy Jim Burton)

Appendix V

Genealogy

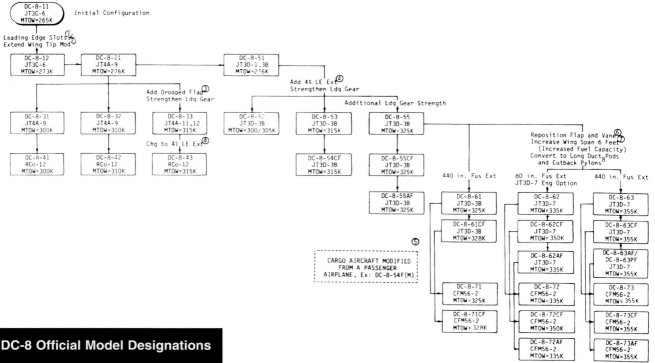

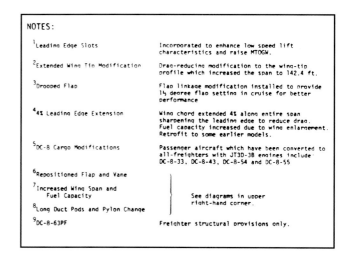

DC-8 Official Model Designations

Model	Date Certified
DC-8-11	August 31, 1959
DC-8-12	July 1, 1960
DC-8-21	January 19, 1960
DC-8-31	March 30, 1960
DC-8-32	February 1, 1960
DC-8-33	November 28, 1960
DC-8-41	March 24, 1960
DC-8-42	April 26, 1960
DC-8-43	February 1, 1961
DC-8-51	October 10, 1961
DC-8-52	May 1, 1961
DC-8-53	April 28, 1961
DC-8F-54	January 29, 1963
DC-8F-55	June 19, 1964
DC-8-55	April 25, 1965
DC-8-61	September 1, 1966
DC-8-61F	June 11, 1967
DC-8-62	April 27, 1967
DC-8-62F	April 9, 1968
DC-8-63	June 29, 1967
DC-8-63F	June 10, 1968
DC-8-71	April 13, 1982
DC-8-71F	April 13, 1982
DC-8-72	September 17, 1982
DC-8-72F	September 17, 1982
DC-8-73	June 23, 1982
DC-8-73F	June 23, 1982

NOTES:

[1] Leading Edge Slots — Incorporated to enhance low speed lift characteristics and raise MTOGW.

[2] Extended Wing Tip Modification — Drag-reducing modification to the wing-tip profile which increased the span to 142.4 ft.

[3] Drooped Flap — Flap linkage modification installed to provide 1½ degree flap setting in cruise for better performance

[4] 4% Leading Edge Extension — Wing chord extended 4% along entire span sharpening the leading edge to reduce drag. Fuel capacity increased due to wing enlargement. Retrofit to some earlier models.

[5] DC-8 Cargo Modifications — Passenger aircraft which have been converted to all-freighters with JT3D-3B engines include: DC-8-33, DC-8-43, DC-8-54 and DC-8-55

[6] Repositioned Flap and Vane
[7] Increased Wing Span and Fuel Capacity — See diagrams in upper right-hand corner.
[8] Long Duct Pods and Pylon Change

[9] DC-8-63PF — Freighter structural provisions only.

Appendix VI
DC-8 PRODUCTION LIST

This table contains data reported to McDonnell Douglas Corp. through January 1996. Where flight hours only are indicated, the aircraft was still reporting monthly activity.

The individual aircraft information which follows is sequenced in order of actual production, by the Line Number (LN). The manufacturer's serial number (MSN) formally identifies the airframe for legal purposes and remains constant throughout its life. A small steel plate, engraved with this number and other data, is permanently affixed to the cockpit bulkhead. (A second plate was issued for aircraft which received Series 70 upgrades, and installed next to the original panel.)

Registration (REGISTR), Airline (A/L), MODEL and Engine (ENG) columns show the status at the time of delivery.

Model numbers include Douglas "in-house" designations (AB, AF, CF, F, JT, L, PF) which are explained in the main text. Early production aircraft, internally designated either DM (Domestic) or OW (Overwater), and are so identified in parentheses.

Delivery dates (DEL) are those on which the aircraft title was transferred to the airline or its lending company. Title transfer is actually recorded at the precise moment when final payment is deposited in the manufacturer's account, allowing insurance liability to be transferred as well.

The Status (STAT) column indicates whether the aircraft is retired (RET), stored (ST) or was written off (W/O). For aircraft still active, the Status and DATE columns are left blank. Retired aircraft dates reflect when Douglas was notified of the status change. In many cases, the final flight pre-dates this, by as much as several years. Flight hours (HOURS) include final figures for DC-8s no longer flying.

Many DC-8s were structurally modified, often with engine upgrades which changed the designation. The current or final model type, if changed from the original configuration, is indicated in the last column (CVTD). Numerous aircraft had interim changes incorporated. For example, Air Canada converted DC-8-63s to -63F layouts before upgrading with CFM-56 engines, which brought them up to model 73Fs.

Airline Abbreviations (A/L) - Original Delivery Customers

AC	Trans-Canada/Air Canada	JL	Japan Air Lines	SA	Saturn Airways
AM	Aeronaves de Mexico/ Aeromexico	IB	Iberia	SB	Seaboard World Airlines
		KL	KLM	SK	SAS-Scandinavian
AT	Atlantis	NA	National Airlines	SR	Swissair
AY	Finnair	NW	Northwest	TC	Trans Caribbean Airways
AZ	Alitalia	OV	ONA-Overseas National Airways	TE	TEAL/Air New Zealand
BN	Braniff International Airways			TV	Trans International/ Transamerica
CG	Air Congo	PA	Pan American World Airways	
CL	Capitol International Airways	PB	Pan Air do Brasil	UA	United
CP	Canadian Pacific/CP Air	PG	Pan American Grace (Panagra)	UT	TAI/UAT/UTA
DL	Delta	QC	Air Zaire	UV	Universal Airlines
EA	Eastern	PR	Philippine Airlines	VA	VIASA
FT	Flying Tigers	RD	Riddle/Airlift International	WO	World Airways
GA	Garuda	RK	Air Afrique	ZF	American Flyers (AFA)

An asterisk (*) follows the Line Number of each aircraft photographically represented in this book.

LN	MSN	REGISTR	A/L	MODEL		ENG	DEL	STAT	HOURS	DATE	CVTD
01*	45252	N8008D	TV	11	(DM)	JT3D-1	06-22-62	ST	60,918	05-24-89	51
02*	45278	N8001U	UA	21	(DM)	JT4A-9	11-01-60	RET	52,058	01-23-78	
03*	45279	N8002U	UA	12	(DM)	JT3C-6	05-11-61	RET	50,043	02-22-78	21
04*	45280	N8003U	UA	11	(DM)	JT3C-6	06-16-60	RET	53,771	04-15-94	21
05*	45253	N800PA	PA	33	(OW)	JT4A-12	06-02-61	W/O	16,776	03-04-67	
06	45254	N801PA	PA	33	(OW)	JT4A-12	04-08-61	RET	43,244	01-01-84	
07	45255	N802PA	PA	33	(OW)	JT4A-12	02-15-61	RET	42,852	06-01-82	
08*	45281	N8004U	UA	11	(DM)	JT3C-6	05-29-59	RET	55,049	01-04-78	21
09*	45442	CF-TJA	AC	41	(OW)	RCo-12	09-25-60	RET	46,661	09-30-82	
10*	45282	N8005U	UA	11	(DM)	JT3C-6	06-27-59	RET	53,986	01-11-78	21
11	45283	N8006U	UA	11	(DM)	JT3C-6	08-19-59	RET	53,774	08-21-78	
12	45284	N8007U	UA	11	(DM)	JT3C-6	08-25-59	RET	61,346	05-21-81	51
13	45285	N8008U	UA	11	(DM)	JT3C-6	09-03-59	RET	66,998	03-02-93	51
14*	45408	N801E	DL	11	(DM)	JT3C-6	07-21-59	RET	53,988	07-21-77	51
15	45286	N8009U	UA	11	(DM)	JT3C-6	09-14-59	RET	60,657	01-01-84	51

LN	MSN	REGISTR	A/L	MODEL		ENG	DEL	STAT	HOURS	DATE	CVTD
16*	45287	N8010U	UA	11	(DM)	JT3C-6	09-29-59	RET	60,829	07-29-81	51
17	45288	N8011U	UA	11	(DM)	JT3C-6	10-22-59	RET	61,651	01-01-84	51
18	45443	CF-TJB	AC	41	(OW)	RC0-12	05-25-60	RET	42,292	01-01-80	
19	45409	N802E	DL	11	(DM)	JT3C-6	09-14-59	W/O	23,390	03-30-67	
20	45289	N8012U	UA	11	(DM)	JT3C-6	12-18-59	RET	54,506	12-15-85	21F
21	45410	N803E	DL	11	(DM)	JT3C-6	10-10-59		61,856		51
22	45290	N8013U	UA	11	(DM)	JT3C-6	12-12-59	W/O	2,433	12-16-60	
23	45411	N804E	DL	11	(DM)	JT3C-6	10-27-59	RET	58,564	08-21-89	51
24*	45412	N805E	DL	11	(DM)	JT3C-6	11-04-59	RET	58,603	09-01-83	51
25	45413	N806E	DL	11	(DM)	JT3C-6	11-11-59	RET	60,831	08-01-86	51
26	45588	N8014U	UA	11	(DM)	JT3C-6	11-18-59	RET	55,131	02-06-78	21
27	45589	N8015U	UA	11	(DM)	JT3C-6	11-21-59	RET	52,618	10-04-82	21
28	45590	N8016U	UA	11	(DM)	JT3C-6	12-02-59	RET	51,407	11-22-77	21
29	45591	N8017U	UA	11	(DM)	JT3C-6	12-05-59	RET	55,378	10-01-81	21
30	45291	N8018U	UA	21	(DM)	JT4A-3	02-28-60	RET	55,483	05-01-78	21
31	45444	CF-TJC	AC	41	(OW)	RCo-12	03-27-60	RET	46,915	05-01-80	
32	45592	N8019U	UA	11	(DM)	JT3C-6	12-30-59	RET	53,829	08-18-78	21
33	45593	N8020U	UA	11	(DM)	JT3C-6	01-14-60	RET	53,217	03-17-78	21
34	45422	N8601	EA	21	(DM)	JT4A-3	01-03-60	RET	39,231	12-20-76	
35	45594	N8021U	UA	21	(DM)	JT4A-3	01-21-60	RET	51,494	06-15-86	21F
36*	45423	N8602	EA	21	(DM)	JT4A-3	01-22-60	RET	40,497	02-26-76	
37	45424	N8603	EA	21	(DM)	JT4A-3	02-14-60	RET	41,149	12-01-87	
38*	45391	N6571C	NA	21	(DM)	JT4A-3	02-07-60	RET	44,986	12-15-84	
39	45595	N8022U	UA	21	(DM)	JT4A-3	02-17-60	RET	54,528	12-15-85	
40	45256	N803PA	PA	32	(OW)	JT4A-5	02-07-60	RET	47,116	02-01-85	33
41	45425	N8604	EA	21	(DM)	JT4A-3	02-19-60	RET	40,059	07-04-77	
42*	45445	CF-TJD	AC	41	(OW)	RCo-12	02-07-60	RET	48,611	07-01-80	
43	45292	N8023U	UA	21	(DM)	JT4A-3	02-26-60	RET	55,099	11-23-77	
44*	45257	N804PA	PA	32	(OW)	JT4A-5	03-17-60	RET	47,010	10-25-88	32F
45	45392	N6572C	NA	21	(DM)	JT4A-3	03-07-60	RET	46,322	02-01-85	
46	45258	N805PA	PA	32	(OW)	JT4A-5	03-20-60	RET	48,975	12-01-87	32F
47	45293	N8024U	UA	21	(DM)	JT4A-3	04-06-60	RET	56,412	10-01-81	
48*	45376	PH-DCA	KL	32	(OW)	JT4A-3	03-19-60	RET	57,468	04-21-81	33
49	46426	N8605	EA	21	(DM)	JT4A-3	04-09-60	RET	38,873	02-22-74	
50*	45384	OY-KTA	SK	32	(OW)	JT4A-3	03-31-60	ST	59,979	02-24-88	33F
51	45294	N8025U	UA	21	(DM)	JT4A-3	04-12-60	RET	56,121	03-06-78	
52*	45274	N8274H	PG	31	(OW)	JT4A-3	04-06-60	RET	50,410	10-24-86	
53	45377	PH-DCB	KL	32	(OW)	JT4A-3	04-18-60	RET	59,206	05-03-95	33F
54*	45416	HB-IDA	SR	32	(OW)	JT4A-3	04-22-60	RET	62,410	01-15-92	33F
55	45385	LN-MOA	SK	32	(OW)	JT4A-3	05-04-60	RET	59,943	01-01-83	33F
56*	45427	N8606	EA	21	(DM)	JT4A-3	04-26-60	RET	40,557	01-01-81	
57*	45598	I-DIWA	AZ	42	(OW)	RCo-12	04-28-60	W/O	49,071	08-01-80	42F
58	45259	N806PA	PA	32	(OW)	JT4A-5	05-07-60	RET	58,754	09-30-92	32F
59	45378	PH-DCC	KL	32	(OW)	JT4A-3	05-09-60	RET	52,358	07-01-80	33
60*	45602	N801US	NW	32	(OW)	JT4A-9	05-18-60	RET	48,511	03-20-79	
61*	45428	N8607	EA	21	(DM)	JT4A-3	05-22-60	W/O	11,340	02-25-64	
62	45386	SE-DBA	SK	32	(OW)	JT4A-3	05-11-60	W/O	56,684	09-11-80	33F
63	45295	N8026U	UA	21	(DM)	JT4A-3	05-17-60	RET	56,985	01-15-84	21F
64*	45275	N8275H	PG	31	(OW)	JT4A-3	05-26-60	RET	31,376	01-01-81	
65	45296	N8027U	UA	21	(DM)	JT4A-9	05-25-60	RET	56,802	01-15-86	21F
66	45260	N807PA	PA	32	(OW)	JT4A-10	06-03-60	RET	49,181	03-12-86	32F
67	45297	N8028U	UA	21	(DM)	JT4A-9	06-08-60	RET	55,631	03-28-78	
68	45261	N808PA	PA	32	(OW)	JT4A-10	06-10-60	RET	51,401	12-01-87	32F
69	45417	HB-IDB	SR	32	(OW)	JT4A-9	06-19-60	RET	76,977	11-07-83	53
70	45262	N809PA	PA	32	(OW)	JT4A-10	06-22-60	RET	48,393	08-01-86	32F
71*	45567	F-BJLA	UT	32	(OW)	JT4A-9	06-27-60	RET	53,325	12-15-84	33
72	45276	N8276H	PG	31	(OW)	JT4A-9	06-29-60	RET	42,784	01-07-82	

LN	MSN	REGISTR	A/L	MODEL		ENG	DEL	STAT	HOURS	DATE	CVTD
73*	45599	I-DIWE	AZ	42	(OW)	RCo-12	07-05-60	RET	48,358	09-22-81	
74	45603	N802US	NW	32	(OW)	JT4A-9	07-03-60	RET	43,718	08-01-90	32F
75*	45379	PH-DCD	KL	32	(OW)	JT4A-9	07-04-60	RET	48,324	10-16-77	33
76	45387	OY-KTB	SK	32	(OW)	JT4A-9	07-13-60	RET	53,298	05-15-87	33F
77	45263	N810PA	PA	32	(OW)	JT4A-10	07-16-60	RET	47,608	06-02-85	32F
78*	45418	JA8001	JL	32	(OW)	JT4A-9	07-16-60	RET	39,348	01-01-75	
79	45600	I-DIWI	AZ	42	(OW)	RCo-12	07-22-60	ST	52,985	12-01-86	42F
80	45569	F-BIUY	UT	32	(OW)	JT4A-9	07-31-60	RET	56,820	12-15-84	33
81*	45419	JA8002	JL	32	(OW)	JT4A-9	07-29-60	RET	38,214	06-19-91	32F
82	45429	N8608	EA	21	(DM)	JT4A-9	08-08-60	RET	42,323	09-18-84	
83*	45568	F-BJLB	UT	32	(OW)	JT4A-9	08-05-60	RET	62,739	09-24-85	53
84*	45604	N803US	NW	32	(OW)	JT4A-9	08-11-60	RET	56,108	11-01-85	53
85	45298	N8029U	UA	21	(DM)	JT4A-9	08-17-60	RET	57,312	06-15-87	21F
86	45264	N811PA	PA	32	(OW)	JT4A-10	08-23-60	RET	48,660	08-01-86	32F
87	45380	PH-DCE	KL	32	(OW)	JT4A-9	08-19-60	RET	52,357	11-01-85	33
88	45596	N8030U	UA	21	(DM)	JT4A-9	08-27-60	RET	52,679	05-10-78	
89	45526	HB-IDC	SR	32	(OW)	JT4A-9	08-29-60	W/O	43,884	05-10-73	33
90	45388	LN-MOT	SK	32	(OW)	JT4A-9	08-31-60	RET	53,382	04-01-86	32F
91*	45265	N812PA	PA	32	(OW)	JT4A-10	09-10-60	RET	41,451	10-01-82	33
92	45299	N8031U	UA	21	(DM)	JT4A-9	09-11-60	RET	53,640	10-01-81	21F
93*	45420	JA8003	JL	32	(OW)	JT4A-9	09-13-60	RET	56,772	09-01-90	53
94	45277	N8277H	PG	31	(OW)	JT4A-9	09-30-60	W/O	26,146	04-28-68	
95	45605	N804US	NW	32	(OW)	JT4A-9	09-22-60	RET	44,390	12-01-75	
96	45381	PH-DCF	KL	32	(OW)	JT4A-9	09-24-60	RET	56,526	10-18-77	33
97	45597	N8032U	UA	21	(DM)	JT4A-9	09-29-60	RET	54,099	10-09-78	
98	45389	SE-DBB	SK	32	(OW)	JT4A-9	09-30-60	RET	58,904	01-01-83	33F
99*	45430	N8609	EA	21	(DM)	JT4A-9	10-09-60	RET	39,138	01-01-81	
100	45266	N813PA	PA	32	(OW)	JT4A-10	10-13-60	RET	40,712	11-19-84	
101	45300	N8033U	UA	21	(DM)	JT4A-9	10-13-60	RET	54,300	09-22-86	
102	45267	N814PA	PA	32	(OW)	JT4A-10	10-18-60	RET	45,194	02-05-93	33F
103*	45431	N8610	EA	21	(DM)	JT4A-9	10-23-60	RET	38,398	12-17-77	
104	45268	N815PA	PA	32	(OW)	JT4A-10	11-07-60	RET	38,060	09-01-94	
105*	45432	XA-XAX	AM	21	(DM)	JT4A-9	10-28-60	W/O	529	01-19-61	
106	45382	PH-DCG	KL	32	(OW)	JT4A-9	10-26-60	RET	54,011	10-28-82	33
107	45601	I-DIWO	AZ	42	(OW)	RCo-12	11-02-60	ST	48,342	10-02-90	43
108	45390	SE-DBC	SK	32	(OW)	JT4A-9	11-11-60	RET	60,727	08-15-86	33F
109	45269	N816PA	PA	32	(OW)	JT4A-10	11-10-60	RET	46,428	11-01-89	33F
110	45433	N8612	EA	21	(DM)	JT4A-9	11-15-60	RET	47,174	12-30-91	21F
111	45565	CF-TJE	AC	42	(OW)	RCo-12	11-17-60	RET	41,015	01-01-81	
112	45270	N817PA	PA	33	(OW)	JT4A-12	12-15-60	W/O	43,436	12-11-77	
113*	45421	JA8005	JL	32	(OW)	JT4A-9	11-23-60	RET	49,911	09-28-89	33F
114	45271	N818PA	PA	33	(OW)	JT4A-12	12-22-60	RET	39,823	09-01-81	
115*	45606	N805US	NW	32	(OW)	JT4A-9	01-04-61	ST	54,572	06-01-85	33F
116	45393	N6573C	NA	21	(DM)	JT4A-9	12-09-60	RET	43,875	10-11-76	
117*	45566	CF-TJF	AC	42	(OW)	RCo-12	12-14-60	RET	44,154	01-24-77	
118*	45272	PP-PDS	PB	33	(OW)	JT4A-12	03-21-61	RET	38,202	02-28-92	33F
119	45609	CF-TJG	AC	42	(OW)	RCo-12	12-22-60	RET	47,220	10-01-80	
120	45383	PH-DCH	KL	53	(OW)	JT3D-1	07-13-61	W/O	23,668	06-29-68	
121	45273	PP-PDT	PB	33	(OW)	JT4A-12	03-21-61	W/O	3,808	08-20-62	
122	45610	CF-TJH	AC	42	(OW)	RCo-12	01-12-61		57,575		54F
123*	45613	PH-DCI	KL	53	(OW)	JT3D-1	04-03-61	RET	65,734	12-01-85	
124	45620	CF-CPF	CP	43	(OW)	RCo-12	02-21-61	RET	74,050	11-06-90	
125	45304	N8037U	UA	12	(DM)	JT3C-6	01-25-61	RET	51,372	04-15-87	21F
126	45614	PH-DCK	KL	53	(OW)	JT3D-1	05-01-61	RET	68,606	12-01-85	
127*	45611	CF-TJI	AC	43	(OW)	RCo-12	02-02-61	W/O	45,261	10-06-76	
128*	45301	N8034U	UA	52	(OW)	JT3D-1	04-30-61	RET	59,817	11-01-87	
129	45305	N8038U	UA	12	(DM)	JT3C-6	02-08-61	RET	49,443	03-17-78	21

LN	MSN	REGISTR	A/L	MODEL		ENG	DEL	STAT	HOURS	DATE	CVTD
130*	45623	CF-CPG	CP	43	(OW)	RCo-12	11-15-61	RET	70,567	05-01-80	
131	45615	PH-DCL	KL	53	(OW)	JT3D-1	05-01-61	W/O	193	05-30-61	
132	45621	CF-CPH	CP	43	(OW)	RCo-12	04-01-61	RET	73,927	11-10-80	
133	45302	N8035U	UA	53	(OW)	JT3D-1	05-18-61	RET	54,984	01-01-84	
134	45570	F-BIUZ	UT	33	(OW)	JT4A-11	02-28-61		56,159		
135	45612	CF-TJJ	AC	43	(OW)	RCo-12	03-22-61	RET	48,822	06-01-81	
136	45617	EC-ARA	IB	52	(OW)	JT3D-1	05-22-61	W/O	31,964	07-06-62	
137	45622	CF-CPI	CP	43	(OW)	RCo-12	05-20-61	RET	73,353	01-27-81	
138	45618	EC-ARB	IB	52	(OW)	JT3D-1	05-27-61	RET	46,642	02-25-92	
139	45624	I-DIWU	AZ	43	(OW)	RCo-12	04-28-61	ST	48,067	10-02-90	
140	45306	N8039U	UA	12	(DM)	JT3C-6	04-11-61	RET	48,006	04-04-78	21
141*	45303	N8036U	UA	52	(OW)	JT3D-1	06-08-61	RET	60,186	01-01-84	
142*	45619	EC-ARC	IB	52	(OW)	JT3D-1	06-19-61	RET	43,146	04-26-90	
143	45626	JA8006	JL	33	(OW)	JT4A-9	05-04-61	RET	46,929	07-15-87	33F
144	45625	I-DIWB	AZ	43	(OW)	RCo-12	05-31-61	W/O	38,575	05-05-72	
145	45627	F-BJUV	UT	33	(OW)	JT4A-11	06-03-61	RET	53,213	10-28-79	
146	45307	N8040U	UA	12	(DM)	JT3C-6	06-16-61	W/O	125	07-11-61	
147	45616	PH-DCM	KL	53	(OW)	JT3D-1	06-24-61	RET	65,021	12-01-85	
148	45434	N8613	EA	21	(DM)	JT4A-9	07-28-61	RET	36,780	01-01-81	
149*	45435	N8614	EA	21	(DM)	JT4A-9	08-15-61	RET	38,552	12-30-91	
150	45436	N8615	EA	21	(DM)	JT4A-9	09-06-61	RET	36,312	07-04-77	
151*	45628	N8780R	TC	51	(DM)	JT3D-1	11-06-61	RET	58,904	06-14-85	
152	45437	N8616	EA	21	(DM)	JT4A-9	10-23-61	RET	42,437	08-01-86	21F
153	45636	I-DIWP	AZ	43	(OW)	RCo-12	11-03-61	ST	44,195	10-02-90	
154	45607	PI-C801	PR	53	(OW)	JT3D-3	02-27-62	RET	60,853	08-01-88	
155*	45608	PH-DCP	KL	53	(OW)	JT3D-3	02-27-62	RET	68,156	04-05-87	
156	45638	CF-TJK	AC	43	(OW)	RCo-12	12-16-61	W/O	42,192	03-18-76	
157	45637	I-DIWR	AZ	43	(OW)	RCo-12	02-01-62		56,405		53F
158	45629	PH-DCN	KL	53	(OW)	JT3D-3	01-17-62	RET	69,584	10-24-85	
159	45630	I-DIWF	AZ	43	(OW)	RCo-12	02-28-62	W/O	21,998	08-02-62	
160	45631	I-DIWD	AZ	43	(OW)	RCo-12	03-24-62	W/O	959	07-06-62	
161	45634	N774C	NA	51	(DM)	JT3D-3	02-23-62	RET	56,218	01-01-86	
162*	4563.	XA-NUS	AM	51	(DM)	JT3D-3	05-10-62	W/O	13,743	12-24-66	
163*	45635	N875C	NA	51	(DM)	JT3D-3	04-06-62		72,293		51F
164	45632	PH-DCO	KL	53	(OW)	JT3D-3	06-27-62		65,125		
165	45461	N276C	NA	51	(DM)	JT3D-3	05-25-62	RET	67,780	08-15-87	
166	45645	N807E	DL	51	(DM)	JT3D-1	04-27-62	RET	51,825	01-15-88	
167*	45646	N808E	DL	51	(DM)	JT3D-1	05-15-62	ST	47,407	06-30-87	
168	45647	JA8007	JL	53	(OW)	JT3D-3	03-27-62	RET	56,811	04-16-86	
169	45648	N8781R	TC	51	(DM)	JT3D-1	07-06-62	RET	51,290	07-01-84	
170	45649	N809E	DL	51	(DM)	JT3D-1	06-20-62		61,226		
171	45659	EC-ASN	IB	52	(OW)	JT3D-3	10-04-62	RET	54,085	10-31-89	
172	45642	N877C	NA	51	(DM)	JT3D-3	09-25-62	RET	54,903	11-02-85	
173	45643	N278C	NA	51	(DM)	JT3D-3	10-23-62	RET	53,624	05-01-86	
174*	45644	N779C	NA	51	(DM)	JT3D-3	11-20-62	RET	53,389	11-01-87	
175*	45640	CF-TJL	AC	54JT		JT3D-3	04-23-63		65,608		
176	45652	XA-PEI	AM	51	(DM)	JT3D-3	11-24-62	W/O	10,126	08-13-66	
177	45650	N810E	DL	51	DM)	JT3D-3	12-12-62	RET	45,058	05-05-76	
178	45653	CF-TJM	AC	54JT		JT3D-3	01-30-63	W/O	9,666	05-20-67	
179	45654	CF-TJN	AC	54JT		JT3D-3	02-08-63	W/O	2,175	11-24-63	
180	45655	CF-TJO	AC	54JT		JT3D-3	02-27-63	RET	55,801	05-16-84	54F
181	45658	EC-ATP	IB	52	(OW)	JT3D-3	03-29-63		49,396		
182*	45669	N8008F	TV	54JT		JT3D-3	04-26-63		64,669		
183*	45661	CF-CPJ	CP	43	(OW)	RCo-12	05-03-63	RET	68,534	11-06-90	
184	45660	I-DIWG	AZ	43	(OW)	RCo-12	05-21-63	RET	43,277	11-14-89	
185*	45667	N8782R	TC	54JT		JT3D-3	06-21-63		63,955		
186	45662	JA8009	JL	53	(OW)	JT3D-3	07-16-63		65,728		

LN	MSN	REGISTR	A/L	MODEL	ENG	DEL	STAT	HOURS	DATE	CVTD
187*	45668	N4904C	CL	54JT	JT3D-3	09-13-63		55,289		
188	45657	EC-AUM	IB	52 (OW)	JT3D-3	08-28-68	RET	42,986	10-25-74	
189*	45663	N108RD	RD	54JT	JT3D-3	09-20-63		65,666		
190	45670	TU-TCA	RK	53 (OW)	JT3D-3B	10-19-63	RET	54,795	04-13-85	
191	45656	HB-IDD	SR	53 (OW)	JT3D-3B	10-29-63	W/O	31,047	09-16-70	
192	45672	N811E	DL	51 (DM)	JT3D-1	11-14-63	RET	48,035	07-17-88	
193	45673	N812E	DL	51 (DM)	JT3D-1	11-30-63	RET	41,197	04-23-76	
194	45665	I-DIWS	AZ	43 (OW)	RCo-12	12-12-63	RET	37,954	06-05-89	
195*	45684	N8783R	TC	54JT	JT3D-3B	12-16-63		60,167		
196*	45671	TU-TCB	RK	53 (OW)	JT3D-3B	01-10-64	RET	55,684	09-24-85	
197	45676	N8042U	UA	54JT	JT3D-3B	01-30-64		55,816		
198	45651	JA8010	JL	53 (OW)	JT3D-3B	01-31-64		62,571		53F
199	45677	N8043U	UA	54JT	JT3D-3B	02-14-64	W/O	50,756	04-28-95	
200	45675	N8041U	UA	54JT	JT3D-3B	03-28-64		55,049		
201*	45674	N109RD	RD	54JT	JT3D-3B	06-17-64	RET	60,048	04-16-84	
202*	45666	I-DIWI	AZ	43 (OW)	RCo-12	04-14-64	ST	39,314	10-02-90	
203	45679	CF-TJP	AC	54JT	JT3D-3B	03-25-64		66,707		54F
204*	45685	XA-PIK	AM	51 (DM)	JT3D-3B	04-30-64	W/0	73,105	05-21-94	51F
205	45688	N813E	DL	51 (DM)	JT3D-1	05-15-64	RET	44,145	11-30-84	
206	45664	JA8011	JL	53 (OW)	JT3D-3B	06-15-64	RET	63.054	08-08-88	
207*	45692	N801SW	SB	55JT	JT8D-3B	06-21-64		62,942		55F
208*	45683	PH-DCS	KL	55JT	JT3D-3B	07-25-64		73,691		
209	45691	PH-DCT	KL	55JT	JT3D-3B	08-15-64	RET	56,141	01-01-84	
210	45686	CF-TJQ	AC	54JT	JT3D-3B	08-27-64		65,731		54F
211	45687	N814E	DL	51 (DM)	JT3D-1	10-28-64	ST	46,346	05-24-89	
212*	45689	N815E	DL	51 (DM)	JT3D-1	11-05-64		53,135		51F
213	45680	JA8012	JL	53 (OW)	JT3D-3B	11-20-64	W/O	28,685	06-14-72	
214	45681	JA8013	JL	53 (OW)	JT3D-3B	01-14-65	W/O	28,143	09-23-72	
215	45769	N8784R	TC	54JT	JT3D-3B	12-11-64	W/O	3,724	10-24-65	
216	45760	N8779R	EA	51 (DM)	JT3D-3B	12-30-64	RET	40,741	01-01-84	
217	45750	ZK-NZA	TE	52 (OW)	JT3D-3B	07-19-65	RET	49,141	11-01-87	
218	45678	JA8014	JL	55JT	JT3D-3B	03-05-65		69,041		
219	45690	N816E	DL	51 (DM)	JT3D-1	03-24-65	RET	41,573	01-30-86	
220	45682	I-DIWL	AZ	43 (OW)	RCo-12	03-12-65	RET	32,958	04-01-85	54F
221	45693	N8060U	UA	52 (DM)	JT3D-3B	04-17-65	RET	45,267	06-15-87	
222*	45755	I-DIWM	AZ	43 (OW)	RCo-12	04-15-65	RET	35,878	11-14-89	
223*	45753	SE-DBD	SK	55 (OW)	JT3D-3B	04-27-65		69,736		
224	45694	N8061U	UA	52 (DM)	JT3D-3B	05-07-65		45,616		
225*	45754	N3325T	TV	55JT	JT3D-3B	05-18-65	W/O	57,006	09-18-84	
226	45757	N8062U	UA	52 (DM)	JT3D-3B	06-15-65	RET	58,243	09-22-92	
227	45758	N8963U	UA	52 (DM)	JR3D-3B	07-02-65	RET	43,381	11-30-84	
228*	45759	N8064U	UA	52 (DM)	JT3D-3B	07-10-65	RET	53,927	10-12-94	
229	45803	N8785R	TC	55JT	JT3D-3B	07-15-65		64,511		
230*	45756	N8065U	UA	52 (DM)	JT3D-3B	07-29-65	RET	43,645	09-27-84	
231	45751	ZK-NZB	TE	52 (OW)	JT3D-3B	08-10-65	W/O	2,275	07-04-66	
232	45762	PI-C802	PR	55JT	JT3D-3B	08-25-65		71,333		55F
233	45752	ZK-NZC	TE	52 (OW)	JT3D-3B	09-17-65	ST	55,380	04-30-91	
234	45800	N8044U	UA	54JT	JT3D-3B	09-11-65	W/O	45,658	01-28-96	
235*	45801	N8045U	UA	54JT	JT3D-3B	09-28-65		51,861		
236	45816	N804SW	SB	55JT	JT3D-3B	09-25-65		59,581		
237	45761	CF-CPK	CP	43 (OW)	RCo-12	10-14-65	W/O	1,775	03-04-66	
238	45819	F-BNLD	UT	55JT	JT3D-3B	09-16-65		60,444		
239	45807	N817E	DL	51DM	JT3D-1	10-28-65	RET	40,417	04-24-91	
240	45768	Y-VC-VID	VA	53AB	JT3D-3B	11-04-65		72,775		54F
241	45763	JA8015	JL	55L	JT3D-3B	11-10-65		51,457		55F
242	45818	N802SW	SB	55JT	JT3D-3B	11-13-65	W/O	35,430	12-04-74	
243	45808	N818E	DL	51 (DM)	JT3D-1	11-23-65	RET	42,830	06-30-89	

LN	MSN	REGISTR	A/L	MODEL	ENG	DEL	STAT	HOURS	DATE	CVTD
244	45805	N4905C	CL	55JT	JT3D-3B	11-30-65		85,473		
245	45806	N819E	DL	51 (DM)	JT3D-1	12-10-65	RET	35,790	01-01-86	
246	45820	F-BLKX	UT	55JT	JT3D-3B	12-31-65		51,214		
247	45802	N8046U	UA	54JT	JT3D-3B	01-12-66		56,311		
248	45817	N805SW	SB	55JT	JT3D-3B	01-12-66		65,298		
249	45815	N820E	DL	51 (DM)	JT3D-1	01-21-66	RET	43,327	08-01-86	
250	45767	LN-MOH	SK	55AB	JT3D-3B	02-08-66		68,683		
251	45764	JA8016	JL	55L	JT3D-3B	02-14-66		52,953		55F
252	45810	N8070U	UA	61	JT3D-3B	05-07-67		79,468		71F
253	45959	PH-DCU	KL	55JT	JT3D-3B	02-26-66	W/O	53,176	04-01-88	
254	45804	OY-KTC	SK	55JT	JT3D-3B	03-19-66		68,988		
255	45821	N803SW	SB	55JT	JT3D-3B	03-17-66		83,790		
256	45860	CF-TJR	AC	54JT	JT3D-3B	03-26-66	W/O	51,675	02-15-92	54F
257*	45850	N8066U	UA	52 (DM)	JT3D-3B	04-01-66	RET	39,674	03-19-84	
258*	45814	EC-BAV	IB	52 (OW)	JT3D-3	04-21-66		35,111		
259	45862	N4906C	CL	55JT	JT3D-3B	04-22-66		52,775		
260	45851	N8067U	UA	52 (DM)	JT3D-3B	04-30-66	RET	36,948	01-15-86	
261	45861	CF-TJS	AC	54JT	JT3D-3B	05-07-66		56,543		54F
262	45811	N8071U	UA	61	JT3D-3B	08-15-67		73,041		71F
263	45852	N8068U	UA	52 (DM)	JT3D-3B	05-18-66	RET	37,313	10-31-89	
264	45809	CF-CPM	CP	53 (OW)	JT3D-3B	05-31-66		67,420		
265	45765	PK-GJD	GA	55L	JT3D-3B	07-19-66	RET	49,148	07-09-93	
266	45853	N8069U	UA	52 (DM)	JT3D-3B	06-16-66	RET	46,931	09-22-92	
267	45824	N851F	OV	55JT	JT3D-3B	06-20-66		53,723		
268	45879	Y-VC-VIC	VA	53AB	JT3D-3B	07-01-66	W/O	47,762	09-18-84	54F
269*	45856	N852F	OV	55JT	JT3D-3B	07-07-66		56,721		
270*	45822	LN-MOO	SK	62	JT3D-3B	06-20-67	W/O	7,034	01-13-69	
271	45857	TU-TCC	RK	55JT	JT3D-3B	08-02-66	RET	45,879	09-06-83	
272	45766	PH-DCV	KL	55L	JT3D-3B	08-19-66	RET	45,900	09-15-87	
273	45877	N821E	DL	51 (DM)	JT3D-3B	08-25-66	RET	42,143	08-30-90	
274*	45858	N1509U	BN	55JT	JT3D-3B	09-02-66	ST	55,696	09-09-93	
275	45880	N8047U	UA	54JT	JT3D-3B	09-09-66	W/O	29,832	12-18-77	
276	45881	N8048U	UA	54JT	JT3D-3B	09-28-66		46,467		
277*	45812	N8072U	UA	61	JT3D-3B	02-17-68		73,706		71F
278	45854	JA8017	JL	55L	JT3D-3B	09-27-66	RET	49,903	02-28-95	
279	45823	SE-DBE	SK	62	JT3D-3B	05-03-67	W/O	12,557	04-19-70	
280	45878	XA-SIA	AM	51 (DM)	JT3D-3B	10-14-66	RET	61,372	04-19-90	
281	45855	XA-SIB	AM	51 (DM)	JT3D-3B	10-21-66		65,691		
282	45882	JA8018	JL	55JT	JT3D-3B	10-26-66	W/O	66,322	02-04-96	
283	45886	N8049U	UA	54JT	T3D-3B	11-10-66		50,740		
284	45813	N8073U	UA	61	JT3D-3B	01-26-67		75,670		71F
285	45848	N8778	EA	61	JT3D-3B	02-23-67		52,485		61F
286	45903	PH-DEA	KL	63	JT3D-3B	11-08-67		59,800		63F
287	45887	N8777	EA	61	JT3D-3B	03-22-67		50,385		61F
288*	45907	N822E	DL	61	JT3D-3B	04-09-67		69,809		71F
289	45849	N8074U	UA	61	JT3D-3B	04-30-67		77,809		71F
290	45888	N8776	EA	61	JT3D-3B	05-16-67		51,318		
291	45889	N8775	EA	61	JT3D-3B	05-28-67	W/O	36,956	02-09-82	
292	45914	N823E	DL	61	JT3D-3B	05-28-67		71,527		71F
293	45901	PH-DEB	KL	63	JT3D-3B	06-11-67		62,563		63F
294*	45902	N8961T	TV	61CF	JT3D-3B	06-16-67		60,526		71CF
295	45915	N824E	DL	61	JT3D-3B	07-19-67		72,189		71F
296*	45908	N45090	NA	61	JT3D-3B	08-06-67		55,299		61F
297	45894	N8774	EA	61	JT3D-3B	08-06-67		48,069		61F
298	45905	SE-DBF	SK	62	JT3D-3B	08-08-67		74,263		
299	45895	N1803	BN	62	JT3D-3B	08-22-67		74,365		
300	45906	OY-KTD	SK	62	JT3D-3B	08-29-67		72,034		62F

LN	MSN	REGISTR	A/L	MODEL	ENG	DEL	STAT	HOURS	DATE	CVTD
301	45890	CF-TJT	AC	61	JT3D-3B	09-13-67		49,641		
302	45916	JA8019	JL	55L	JT3D-3B	09-18-67	RET	45,010	08-05-86	
303	45896	N1804	BN	62	JT3D-3B	09-20-67		64,789		
304*	45899	N1805	BN	62	JT3D-3B	09-29-67		74,551		
305	45891	CF-TJU	AC	61	JT3D-3B	10-04-67		50,331		61F
306	45892	CF-TJV	AC	61	JT3D-3B	10-14-67		45,010		61F
307	45909	I-DIWN	AZ	62	JT3D-3B	10-28-67		68,058		62F
308	45883	N806SW	SB	55JT	JT3D-3B	10-20-67		59,523		
309	45904	N1807	BN	62CF	JT3D-3B	11-13-67	ST	72,544	10-14-93	
310*	45893	CF-TJW	AC	61	JT3D-3B	11-04-67		50,851		
311	45910	I-DIWV	AZ	62	JT3D-3B	11-16-67		44,510		
312	45919	HB-IDE	SR	62	JT3D-3B	11-23-67	W/O	46,419	10-08-79	
313	45897	N8786R	TC	61CF	JT3D-3B	12-06-67		60,660		71CF
314	45940	N8075U	UA	61	JT3D-3B	12-08-67		52,566		61F
315*	45912	N8771	EA	61	JT3D-3B	12-09-67		52,692		
316*	45900	N8962T	TV	61CF	JT3D-3B	11-30-67		60,296		71CF
317*	45941	N8076U	UA	61	JT3D-3B	12-23-67		72,981		71F
318	45911	N1806	BN	62	JT3D-3B	12-19-67		64,669		62CF
319*	45920	HB-IDF	SR	62	JT3D-3B	01-02-68		72,814		
320	45898	N8787R	TC	61CF	JT3D-3B	12-28-67		60,319		71CF
321	45948	N8955U	SA	61CF	JT3D-3B	12-28-67		60,544		71CF
322	45921	SE-DBG	SR	62	JT3D-3B	01-11-68		80,543		
323	45926	CF-CPO	CP	63	JT3D-3B	01-17-68		80,422		
324	45937	PI-C803	PR	53 (OW)	JT3D-3B	01-27-68	W/O	35,807	04-19-77	
325*	45913	N8770	EA	61	JT3D-3B	01-19-68	ST	49,302	06-01-89	
326	45944	N825E	DL	61	JT3D-3B	01-24-68		69,538		71CF
327	45927	CF-CPP	CP	63	JT3D-3B	01-31-68		77,572		
328	45932	ZK-NZD	TE	52 (OW)	JT3D-3B	01-27-68		61,466		54F
329*	45949	N8956U	SA	61CF	JT3D-3B	01-30-68		58,553		71CF
330	45935	XA-SID	AM	51 (DM)	JT3D-3B	02-07-68		61,447		
331	45938	N8960T	TV	61CF	JT3D-3B	02-02-68		60,013		71CF
332	45917	F-BNLE	UT	62	JT3D-3B	02-23-68		59,461		62F
333	45925	HB-IDG	SR	62	JT3D-3B	02-24-68		76,127		
334*	45928	CF-CPQ	CP	63	JT3D-3B	02-24-68		75,633		
335*	45922	OY-KTE	SR	62CF	JT3D-3B	02-29-68		64,129		
336*	45985	ZK-NZE	TE	52 (OW)	JT3D-3B	02-27-68		52,536		
337	45945	N8077U	UA	61	JT3D-3B	03-05-68		73,068		71F
338	45952	N8788R	TC	61CF	JT3D-3B	02-29-68		54,199		71CF
339*	45946	N8078U	UA	61	JT3D-3B	03-14-68		71,361		71F
340	45884	N8050U	UA	54JT	JT3D-3B	03-12-68		45,538		
341	45947	N8079U	UA	61	JT3D-3B	03-21-68		77,706		71F
342	45885	N8051U	UA	54JT	JT3D-3B	03-19-68		38,304		
343	45970	N8080U	UA	61	JT3D-3B	03-29-68		79,756		71F
344	45936	N8631	SB	63CF	JT3D-3B	06-21-68		87,909		73CF
345	45982	N8769	EA	61	JT3D-3B	03-29-68	W/O	49,276	07-11-91	
346*	45965	EC-BMV	IB	55JT	JT3D-3B	03-31-68		41,297		
347	45960	I-DIWC	AZ	62CF	JT3D-3B	04-10-68		57,618		
348*	45953	JA8031	JL	62	JT3D-3B	04-19-68		64,115		
349	45942	N8773	EA	61	JT3D-3B	04-12-68		44,329		
350*	45983	N8768	EA	61	JT3D-3B	04-19-68		60,132		71F
351	45939	N801U	UV	61CF	JT3D-3B	04-18-68		60,026		71CF
352*	45981	N45191	NA	61	JT3D-3B	04-23-68		54,153		61F
353	45918	F-BOLF	UT	62	JT3D-3B	04-27-68		70,441		62F
354	45950	N802U	UV	61CF	JT3D-3B	04-26-68		60,956		71CF
355	45963	CF-TJX	AC	61	JT3D-3B	04-29-68		42,873		
356*	45971	N8081U	UA	61	JT3D-3B	05-12-68		73,451		71F
357	45972	N8082U	UA	61	JT3D-3B	05-22-68	W/O	33,108	12-28-78	

LN	MSN	REGISTR	A/L	MODEL	ENG	DEL	STAT	HOURS	DATE	CVTD
358	45973	N8083U	UA	61	JT3D-3B	05-20-68		64,359		71F
359*	45943	N8772	EA	61	JT3D-3B	05-19-68		50,660		
360	45992	N8767	EA	61	JT3D-3B	05-21-68		43,615		61F
361*	45961	I-DIWQ	AZ	62CF	JT3D-3B	06-30-68		58,190		
362	45954	JA8032	JL	62	JT3D-3B	05-27-68		57,949		62F
363	45979	N826E	DL	61	JT3D-3B	05-30-68		67,254		71F
364*	45964	CF-TJY	AC	61	JT3D-3B	05-30-68		49,778		61F
365	45955	JA8033	JL	62	JT3D-3B	06-10-68		59,102		62CF
366	45987	F-BOLG	UT	62	JT3D-3B	06-14-68		69,773		62F
367	45929	CF-CPS	CP	63	JT3D-3B	06-16-68	W/O	77,096	02-16-95	
368	45974	N8084U	UA	61	JT3D-3B	06-21-68		66,477		71F
369	45975	N8085U	UA	61	JT3D-3B	06-25-68		66,037		71F
370*	45984	HB-IDH	SR	62CF	JT3D-3B	07-11-68		56,096		
371	45989	N779FT	FT	63CF	JT3D-7	06-28-68		77,809		
372	45976	N8086U	UA	61	JT3D-3B	07-10-68		71,157		71F
373	45977	N8087U	UA	61	JT3D-3B	07-16-68		69,428		71F
374	45980	CF-TJZ	AC	61	JT3D-3B	07-13-68		41,853		61F
375*	45990	N780FT	FT	63CF	JT3D-7	07-17-77		71,128		73CF
376	45956	JA8034	JL	62	JT3D-3B	07-19-68		62,650		62CF
377*	45999	PH-DEC	KL	63	JT3D-7	07-21-68		72,943		
378	45930	EC-BMX	IB	63	JT3D-7	08-08-68	W/O	30,137	03-03-78	
379	45986	I-DIWJ	AZ	62	JT3D-3B	07-26-68		45,351		
380	45991	N781FT	FT	63CF	JT3D-7	07-26-68		81,718		73CF
381	45978	N8088U	UA	61	JT3D-3B	07-31-68		73,254		71F
382	45993	N8089U	UA	61	JT3D-3B	08-06-68		69,697		71F
383*	45923	LN-MOU	SK	63	JT3D-7	08-16-68	W/O	70,430	02-15-92	
384	45933	CF-TIH	AC	53 (OW)	JT3D-3B	08-13-68	RET	31,677	07-01-80	
385	45967	N4907C	CL	63CF	JT3D-7	08-20-68		75,106		73CF
386	46000	PH-DED	KL	63	JT3D-7	08-20-68		59,523		63F
387*	45994	N8090U	UA	61	JT3D-3B	08-27-68		75,563		71F
388	45995	N8091U	UA	61	JT3D-3B	09-04-68		75,783		71F
389*	45968	N4908C	CL	63CF	JT3D-70	8-29-68		67,210		73CF
390	45934	CF-TII	AC	53 (OW)	JT3D-3B	08-30-68	RET	33,462	07-01-80	
391	45931	EC-BMY	IB	63	JT3D-7	09-18-68		60,899		
392*	45924	SE-DBH	SK	63	JT3D-7	09-18-68		80,614		63F
393	45966	N8632	SB	63CF	JT3D-7	09-16-68		77,147		73CF
394	46002	N782FT	FT	63CF	JT3D-7	09-17-68		70,927		73CF
395*	46001	N863F	OV	63CF	JT3D-7	09-23-68		69,140		73CF
396	45969	N6161A	RD	63CF	JT3D-7	09-25-68		74,497		
397*	45996	N8092U	UA	61	JT3D-3B	10-01-68		79,678		71F
398	45997	N8093U	UA	61	JT3D-3B	10-08-68		76,137		71F
399	45998	N8094U	UA	61	JT3D-3B	10-22-68		75,048		71F
400	46014	N1300L	DL	61	JT3D-3B	10-18-68		67,659		71F
401	46003	N783FT	FT	63AF	JT3D-7	10-22-68		79,782		73F
402	45962	CF-TIJ	AC	53 (OW)	JT3D-3B	10-16-68	W/O	14,276	06-21-73	
403	46004	N784FT	FT	63AF	JT3D-7	10-25-68		68,612		73F
404	46009	N8052U	UA	54JT	JT3D-3B	10-31-68		38,591		
405	46015	N8766	EA	61	JT3D-3B	11-01-68		47,841		61F
406	46010	N8053U	UA	54JT	JT3D-3B	11-07-68	W/O	31,902	01-11-83	
407	46023	JA8035	JL	62	JT3D-3B	11-11-68		71,175		
408	46011	N8054U	UA	54JT	JT3D-3B	11-11-68		36,503		
409*	46016	N8785	EA	61	JT3D-3B	11-15-68		51,802		
410	46012	N8055U	UA	54JT	JT3D-3B	11-23-68		53,873		
411	46019	PH-DEE	KL	63	JT3D-7	11-27-68		63,442		73F
412	45005	N785FT	FT	63AF	JT3D-7	11-25-68	W/O	6,047	07-26-70	
413	46006	N786FT	FT	63AF	JT3D-7	12-03-68		65,490		73F
414	45951	N4863T	TV	63CF	JT3D-7	11-22-68	W/O	7,878	09-08-70	

LN	MSN	REGISTR	A/L	MODEL	ENG	DEL	STAT	HOURS	DATE	CVTD
415	46020	N8633	SB	63CF	JT3D-7	11-27-68	W/O	41,229	11-15-78	
416	45988	EC-BMZ	IB	63CF	JT3D-7	12-16-68		62,116		
417	46022	JA8036	JL	62AF	JT3D-3B	12-13-68		69,901		
418*	46017	N8764	EA	61	JT3D-3B	12-17-68		46,816		61F
419	46037	N8763	EA	61	JT3D-3B	12-19-68		50,475		
420	46018	N1301L	DL	61	JT3D-3B	12-19-68		63,643		71F
421*	46042	YV-C-VIA	VA	63	JT3D-7	12-22-68		66,583		63F
422	46007	N787FT	FT	63AF	JT3D-7	01-03-69		66,640		73F
423	46008	N788FT	FT	63AF	JT3D-7	01-06-69		67,376		73F
424*	46021	N8634	SB	63CF	JT3D-7	01-09-69	W/O	3,442	10-16-69	
425	46029	N1302L	DL	61	JT3D-3B	01-16-69		67,060		71F
426	46030	N1303L	DL	61	JT3D-3B	01-22-69		65,756		71F
427*	46013	OH-LFR	AY	62CF	JT3D-3B	01-27-69		65,377		72CF
428	46024	JA8037	JL	62	JT3D-3B	01-27-69		59,547		62F
429*	46038	N8762	EA	61	JT3D-3B	02-03-69	ST	44,491	04-15-91	
430	46050	N8635	SB	63CF	JT3D-7	01-30-69	W/O	28,395	03-04-77	
431	46033	CF-TIK	AC	63	JT3D-7	02-15-69		65,233		73F
432*	46044	N790FT	FT	63AF	JT3D-7	02-28-69		77,514		73F
433*	46058	N8759	EA	63PF	JT3D-7	02-24-69	W/O	50,872	12-12-85	
434	46034	CF-TIL	AC	63	JT3D-7	02-16-69		56,696		
435	46031	JA8038	JL	61	JT3D-3B	02-20-69		48,748		61F
436*	46032	JA8039	JL	61	JT3D-3B	02-25-69		46,788		
437	46027	I-DIWV	AZ	62	JT3D-3B	02-26-69		56,367		
438	46035	CF-TIM	AC	63	JT3D-7	02-27-69		55,315		
439	46041	OY-KTF	SR	63	JT3D-7	02-28-69		80,132		63F
440	46051	N8636	SB	63CF	JT3D-7	02-28-69		66,915		73CF
441	46045	N791FT	FT	63CF	JT3D-7	03-17-69		72,095		73CF
442	46052	N8637	SB	63CF	JT3D-7	03-11-69		52,905		73CF
443	46043	OH-LFS	AY	62CF	JT3D-3B	03-22-69		48,597		72CF
444*	46046	N792FT	FT	63CF	JT3D-7	03-21-69		74,488		73CF
445	46036	CF-TIN	AC	63	JT3D-7	03-27-69		54,759		
446*	46053	N8638	SB	63CF	JT3D-7	03-28-69	ST	31,756	09-02-82	73CF
447	46047	N793FT	FT	63CF	JT3D-7	03-31-69		79,340		73CF
448*	46039	N8095U	UA	61	JT3D-3B	05-14-69		71,464		71F
449	46040	N8096U	UA	61	JT3D-3B	05-14-69		66,368		71F
450	46048	N1304L	DL	61	JT3D-3B	04-24-69		66,090		71F
451*	46076	CF-TIO	AC	63	JT3D-7	04-19-69		67,092		73F
452	46026	I-DIWZ	AZ	62	JT3D-3B	04-30-69	W/O	5,982	09-15-70	
453*	46054	LN-MOY	SR	63	JT3D-7	04-26-69		74,993		63F
454*	46087	N864F	OV	63CF	JT3D-7	04-28-69		66,854		
455*	46067	N8966U	UA	62	JT3D-7	06-22-69		38,122		72
456	46059	N4864T	TV	63CF	JT3D-7	06-25-69		72,652		73CF
457*	46063	YV-C-VIB	VA	63	JT3D-7	05-09-69		74,695		73
458*	46082	I-DIWK	AZ	62	JT3D-3B	05-14-69		46,303		72
459*	46064	N8097U	UA	61	JT3D-3B	05-23-69		73,661		71F
460	46065	N8098U	UA	61	JT3D-3B	06-04-69		71,230		71F
461*	46028	F-BOLH	UT	62	JT3D-3B	05-24-69		57,924		62F
462*	46066	N8099U	UA	61	JT3D-3B	06-16-69		71,894		71F
463*	46068	N8967U	UA	62	JT3D-7	06-15-69		46,967		62F
464*	46088	N865F	OV	63CF	JT3D-7	05-29-69		70,361		
465*	46069	N8968U	UA	62	JT3D-7	07-08-69		57,667		62F
466	46080	PH-DEF	KL	63	JT3D-7	06-20-69		61,030		73F
467	46070	N8969U	UA	62	JT3D-7	07-16-69		58,855		
468*	46074	N8760	EA	63PF	JT3D-7	06-21-69		70,824		73F
469	46071	N8970U	UA	62	JT3D-7	07-28-69		50,380		
470*	46077	HB-IDI	SR	62	JT3D-3B	07-05-69		61,532		62F
471*	46081	N8971U	UA	62	JT3D-7	08-11-69		38,704		72

LN	MSN	REGISTR	A/L	MODEL	ENG	DEL	STAT	HOURS	DATE	CVTD
472	46060	N4909C	CL	63CF	JT3D-7	07-02-69	W/O	4,944	11-27-70	
473*	46084	N8972U	UA	62	JT3D-7	08-19-69	ST	42,906	04-29-95	72
474	46057	JA8040	JL	62	JT3D-3B	07-18-69	W/O	11,825	11-28-72	
475*	46078	HB-IDK	SR	62CF	JT3D-3B	08-06-69		46,737		
476*	46079	EC-BQS	IB	63	JT3D-7	08-02-69		63,663		
447	46072	N1305L	DL	61	JT3D-3B	08-08-69		62,121		71F
478	46086	N794FT	FT	63CF	JT3D-7	08-04-69		73,781		73CF
479*	46049	N8639	SB	63CF	JT3D-7	08-08-69		76,028		
480	46061	N6162A	RD.	63CF	JT3D-7	08-20-69		67,445		
481*	46085	N8973U	UA	62	JT3D-7	09-04-69		55,608		
482	46094	N4910C	CL	63CF	JT3D-7	08-15-69		68,183		73CF
483	46103	N795FT	FT	63CF	JT3D-7	08-29-69		75,435		
484	46075	PH-DEH	KL	63	JT3D-7	08-29-69		68,251		
485*	46073	N4865T	TV	63CF	JT3D-7	08-22-67		70,984		73CF
486	46062	N6163A	RD	63CF	JT3D-7	09-15-69		73,189		73CF
487*	46110	N8974U	UA	62	JT3D-7	09-23-69		45,380		
488	46104	N796FT	FT	63CF	JT3D-7	10-03-69		74,956		73CF
489*	46101	N8630	SB	63CF	JT3D-7	09-25-69		79,095		73CF
490*	46106	N8641	SB	63CF	JT3D-7	10-02-69		81,016		73CF
491	46111	N8975U	UA	62	JT3D-7	10-14-69		32,586		
492	46055	N1306L	DL	61	JT3D-3B	11-05-69		61,950		71F
493	46109	N9642	SB	63CF	JT3D-7	10-23-69		68,934		73CF
494	46105	N1808E	BN	62	JT3D-3B	10-23-69		62,265		62F
495	46056	N1307L	DL	61	JT3D-3B	11-06-69		62,977		71F
496*	46093	N8758	EA	63PF	JT3D-7	11-06-69		64,594		63F
497	46095	N8757	EA	63PF	JT3D-7	11-15-69		60,453		73F
498	46107	N1809E	BN	62	JT3D-3B	11-17-69	W/O	52,706	06-07-89	
499	46096	N8756	EA	63PF	JT3D-7	11-21-69	W/O	44,165	03-10-84	
500*	46121	PH-DEL	KL	63	JT3D-7	11-25-69		75,427		63F
501*	46089	N4866T	TV	63CF	JT3D-7	12-29-69		70,510		73CF
502	46100	CF-TIP	AC	63	JT3D-7	12-11-69		62,232		73F
503*	46097	N8755	EA	63PF	JT3D-7	12-14-69		65,031		
504	46090	N4867T	TV	63CF	JT3D-7	12-29-69		70,568		73CF
505	46092	PH-DEG	KL	63	JT3D-7	12-23-69		54,315		63F
506	46122	PH-DEL	KL	63	JT3D-7	12-31-69		65,031		
507*	46099	JA8041	JL	61	JT3D-3B	01-15-70		49,303		71
508*	46123	CF-TIQ	AC	63	JT3D-7	02-04-70		65,321		73F
509	46136	SE-DBK	SK	63	JT3D-7	01-13-70		77,377		
510	46127	JA8042	JL	61	JT3D-3B	02-02-70	W/O	43,947	08-18-93	
511	46124	CF-TIR	AC	63	JT3D-7	02-05-70		64,730		73F
512	46102	LN-MOG	SK	62	JT3D-3B	01-30-70	RET	58,822	03-07-94	
513	46134	HB-IDL	SR	62	JT3D-3B	02-06-70		59,063		62F
514	46128	JA8043	JL	61	JT3D-3B	02-24-70	W/O	27,981	01-15-81	
515	46125	CF-TIS	AC	63	JT3D-7	02-27-70		64,025		73F
516*	46098	I-DIWW	AZ	62	JT3D-3B	02-10-70		41,361		
517*	46131	LN-MOW	SK	62	JT3D-3B	02-25-70		61,240		
518*	46116	EC-BSD	IB	63	JT3D-7	12-23-70		60,149		
519*	46091	N4868T	TV	63CF	JT3D-7	04-15-70		74,893		73CF
520	46112	N866F	OV	63CF	JT3D-7	04-08-70		67,702		73CF
521	46113	CF-TIU	AC	63	JT3D-7	03-12-70		50,927		63F
522*	46108	N123AF	ZF	63CF	JT3D-7	04-24-70		70,053		73CF
523	46129	SE-DBI	SK	62CF	JT3D-3B	04-06-70		61,236		
524*	46126	CF-TIV	AC	63	JT3D-7	04-02-70		48,995		63F
525	46117	N4869T	TV	63CF	JT3D-7	05-15-70		72,087		73CF
526	46114	CF-TIW	AC	63	JT3D-7	04-30-70	W/O	452	07-05-70	
527*	46137	D-ADIX	AT	63CF	JT3D-7	04-29-70		59,885		
528*	46140	N124AF	ZF	63CF	JT3D-7	05-19-70		63,203		73CF

LN	MSN	REGISTR	A/L	MODEL	ENG	DEL	STAT	HOURS	DATE	CVTD
529	46155	EC-BSE	IB	63 P	JT3D-7	12-23-70		61,840		
530	46115	CF-TIX	AC	63	JT3D-7	05-23-70		62,715		
531*	46135	TU-TCF	RK	63CF	JT3D-7	05-28-70		68,674		
532	46144	N6164A	RD	63CF	JT3D-7	06-26-70	W/O	16,832	03-26-74	
533*	46141	PH-DEM	KL	63	JT3D-7	06-20-70		58,261		
534*	46133	N801WA	WO	63CF	JT3D-7	03-19-71		72,122		73CF
535	46132	I-DIWH	AZ	62	JT3D-3B	07-24-70		60,017		
536	46146	N802WA	WO	63CF	JT3D-3B	03-21-71	W/O	10,084	09-08-73	
537	46139	JA8044	JL	62AF	JT3D-3B	09-14-70		66,810		
538	46149	N803WA	WO	63CF	JT3D-7	03-29-71		43,646		73CF
539	46150	LN-MOC	SK	62AF	JT3D-3B	10-22-70		54,377		
540*	46151	9Q-CLG	CG	63CF	JT3D-7	11-09-70		34,093		
541	46157	JA8045	JL	61	JT3D-3B	12-04-70		46,296		61F
542	46130	OH-LFY	AY	62CF	JT3D-3B	12-29-70		58,454		72CF
543	46158	JA8046	JL	61	JT3D-3B	01-20-71		44,153		61F
544	46159	JA8047	JL	61	JT3D-3B	02-18-71		42,890		
545	46160	JA8048	JL	61	JT3D-3B	03-12-71	W/O	26,339	09-17-82	
546	46142	I-DIWX	AZ	62	JT3D-3B	03-12-71		58,097		
547	46143	D-ADIY	AT	63CF	JT3D-7	04-15-71		56,756		
548	46145	D-ADIZ	AT	63CF	JT3D-7	05-26-71		60,427		
549	46147	9Q-CLH	CG	63CF	JT3D-7	07-19-71		39,016		
550	46152	JA8051	JL	62	JT3D-3B	08-23-71	W/O	19,266	09-27-77	
551	46153	JA8052	JL	62	JT3D-3B	10-05-71		56,797		
552	46161	JA8053	JL	62	JT3D-3B	11-13-71	W/O	50,146	03-12-91	62F
553	46148	JA8054	JL	62AF	JT3D-3B	01-10-72	W/O	19,655	01-13-77	
554	46154	JA8055	JL	62AF	JT3D-3B	02-17-72		65,934		
555	46162	JA8056	JL	62AF	JT3D-3B	03-21-72		63,847		
556	46163	SE-DBL	SK	63	JT3D-7	05-12-72		67,648		63F

BIBLIOGRAPHY

Books

Cearley, George W. Jr. *Douglas DC-8*. Dallas, Texas: Privately published, 1992.

Davies, R.E.G. *A History of the World's Airlines*. Oxford University Press, 1967. ISBN No. 0 370000323.

—. *Airlines of the United States Since 1914*. London. England: Putnam, 1972.

—. *Airlines of Latin America*. Washington, D.C.: Smithsonian Institution Press, 1984. ISBN No. 0-8138-1834-6.

Eastwood, A.B. & Roach, J.R. Jet Airliner Production List, Vol.. 2. Middlesex, England: The Aviation Hobby Shop, 1995. ISBN No. O 90717857X.

Gero, David. *Aviation Disasters — The world's major civil airliner crashes since 1950*. Avon, England: Bath Press, 1994. ISBN No. 1-85260-379-8.

Hubler. R.G. *Big Eight — A Biography of an Airplane*. New York: Duell, Sloan & Pearce, 1960. LCCN 60-12830.

Morrison, Wilbur H. *Donald W. Douglas — A Heart With Wings*. Ames, Iowa: Iowa State University Press, 1991.

Nash, H.J.; Sievers, Harry; Whittle, John *The McDonnell Douglas DC-8*. Peterborough, England: Air Britain, 1972

Periodicals

DC-8 Flying Time. Douglas Aircraft Co. Product Support, 1995-1996.

DC-8 Hand Book. Douglas Aircraft Co. Sales Engineering, 1982.

The DC-8 Story. Douglas Aircraft Co. Sales Engineering, 1972.

Advanced DC-8. Douglas Aircraft Co. Sales Engineering, 1965.

Douglas DC-8 Comparison. Douglas Aircraft Co. Sales Engineering, 1965.

DC-8-60 Series Excellence Through Evolution. Douglas Sales Engineering, 1969

Flight Testing the Super Sixties. Douglas Aircraft Co. Flight Test Dept.., 1967.

The Versatile Super 70. Cammacorp, 1982

The Douglas Jet Transport DC-8. Douglas Aircraft Co., Santa Monica, 1953.

DC-8 Operation Manuals. (various).

DC-8 Type Specifications (various), Douglas Aircraft Co. Engineering

DC-8 Assignment To Ramp Schedule. Douglas Aircraft Co., 1972.

The following magazines and periodicals were sources of additional information:

ACAR International-Airline & Commercial Aircraft Report*; *The Aeroplane; American Aviation;* Journal of the *American Aviation Historical Society; Aviation Age; Aviation Daily; Aviation Air Letter; Aviation-Letter*; Aviation Week & Space Technology; Flight International; Flying; Long Beach Press Telegram; Los Angeles Times; Speednews; Western Aviation; World Airline Fleets Monthly News*.

* - Sources of DC-8 individual aircraft histories, reviews, and monthly activity updates.